Barry,
I hope that
reading this book inspires
you as much as writing it
has inspired me. Jack Hamilton

D1040487

CONFLICT—
THE UNEXPECTED GIFT

Making the Most of
Disputes in Life and Work

Jack Hamilton
Elisabeth Seaman
Sharlene Gee
Hillary Freeman

iUniverse, Inc.
Bloomington

CONFLICT—THE UNEXPECTED GIFT
MAKING THE MOST OF DISPUTES IN LIFE AND WORK

iUniverse Star
an iUniverse LLC imprint

iUniverse books may be ordered through booksellers or by contacting:

iUniverse
1663 Liberty Drive
Bloomington, IN 47403
www.iuniverse.com
1-800-Authors (1-800-288-4677)

ISBN: 978-1-9389-0864-4 (sc)
ISBN: 978-1-9389-0865-1 (e)

Library of Congress Control Number: 2014904717

Printed in the United States of America

iUniverse rev. date: 4/7/2014

This groundbreaking book shows how moments of breakdown can be used as opportunities for breakthrough. The authors have written a clear guide to understanding our own assumptions in conflict situations and how to make sure they are valid. The book's tool kit and readability will not only preserve endangered relationships, it will enhance our communities by strengthening our families and work relationships.

—Fred Luskin, PhD, director, associate professor, Stanford Forgiveness Projects; professor, Sofia University; author of *Forgive for Good; Forgive for Love;* and *Stress Free for Good* (with Kenneth R. Pelletier)

How did this conflict happen? How can I address it? What can I do to benefit from it? Many of us have these questions when we find ourselves in an interpersonal conflict. The authors have produced a succinct and practical guide to address conflict successfully. Mastering their easy-to-follow method will change your life. This book will help you lay defensive reactions aside and make your conflicts work for you.

—Marvin L. Schwartz, JD, mediator and trainer of more than two thousand mediators

Conflict—The Unexpected Gift uses a simple analogy, a ladder, to outline a useful process for turning conflict into beneficial discussions. The authors use real life stories to demonstrate how to apply simple techniques to resolve a myriad of everyday disputes.

—Nancy Neal Yeend, dispute management specialist, partner, Y&D Programs, LLC.

This very well-written book describes the key principles of effective conflict management in an easy-to-understand and engaging manner and provides the reader with practical tools for applying those principles in everyday conflicts.

—Patricia Brown, former executive director, Peninsula Conflict Resolution Center, San Mateo, California

As a manager of mediation programs, as well as a mediator and trainer, I recommend Conflict—The Unexpected Gift *for its insights on improving human behavior in a conflict context. I particularly appreciate the tools in this book, such as concrete steps for focusing on positive conflict-resolution attitudes and effective listening. This book will be a useful addition to any teaching and learning library.*

—Martin Eichner, director of dispute resolution programs, Project Sentinel, Inc.

TABLE OF CONTENTS

ACKNOWLEDGMENTS

We owe a great deal to those we've worked with for allowing us to include conflicts from their lives that illustrate key dimensions of our conflict-resolution approach.

We have been guided by insights from our professional training and experience—originally in mediation, psychology, research in counseling methods, high-tech businesses, curriculum development, and conflict management. However, our approach toward conflict resolution has been strongly influenced by ideas from a number of other fields. This book relies heavily on the work of experts from the disciplines of communication management, emotional intelligence, marriage and family therapy, organizational behavior, social intelligence, and social psychology.

We are grateful to Chris Argyris and Peter Senge. Their explorations into miscommunications, stumbling blocks in organizations, and how to train individuals to move beyond them have improved our understanding of how to resolve conflicts. Argyris's work is one of the sources of our Ladder of Assumptions, which we present in chapter 1, and is a major teaching tool in this book. Argyris originated "the

Ladder of Inference," which tracked the way a person takes observations and pairs them with speculation to reach a conclusion that can create a potentially destructive action.

We liked the idea of a ladder but needed one that was more relevant to the people who approached us. So we created the Ladder of Assumptions. It has fewer rungs, and each rung represents a readily identifiable mental process.

The major source for our explanation of the various dimensions of self-awareness in chapter 2 is Daniel Goleman's innovative account of "emotional intelligence," in which he drew upon current brain and behavioral research.

For our work in developing the four components of Listening for Understanding presented in chapter 3, we are especially indebted to three people: Carl Rogers for his pioneering efforts in developing active-listening techniques for counselors; Thomas Gordon for his groundbreaking application of these techniques in his parent effectiveness training methodology; and Mark Brady for his insights into the key role of skillful listening in the human maturation process.

By articulating his novel theory on the positive effects of happenstance in people's lives, John Krumboltz paved the way for us to present a solid argument that conflict is often a gift for individuals at loggerheads with one another.

Peter Pearson, a founder of the Couples Institute, has helped us understand the emotional impediments to changing entrenched behaviors and how people can learn to overcome such blocks.

We owe a debt to Doug Stone, Bruce Patton, and Sheila Heen of the Harvard Negotiation Project for articulating the skills of expression people from vastly different backgrounds need to learn to communicate effectively.

We are indebted to our many colleagues for their detailed feedback on preliminary drafts of the manuscript and to our editor, Gwynne Young, whose insight and intelligence made this a far better book than it otherwise would have been.

Lastly, we treasure our family members and close friends who supported us through the more than three years it has taken to complete this project.

INTRODUCTION

*Even the best of friends face conflicts, but that
needn't mean the end of the relationship.*

—*Reader's Digest*

At some point in your life, you have been entangled in a conflict with another person, whether it was a small disagreement with a store clerk or a full-scale battle with a family member. You may even have managed to find yourself in a conflict—perhaps small and petty but nevertheless a conflict—in the past twenty-four hours.

Conflict is a natural dimension of human interactions. The rough edges of people's personalities can irritate others. When that happens, it leads to clashes among people who live or work together, which often leaves personal relationships damaged.

These standoffs don't need to create a lifetime of hurt and anger. The capacity to learn how to resolve interpersonal conflicts is deeply rooted in our human potential. It may be one of the most valuable skill sets we can develop over the course of our lives.

All told, the four of us have mediated hundreds of cases involving conflicts between adolescent children and parents; adult children and aging parents; husbands and wives; landlords and tenants; employees and managers; coworkers in commercial businesses and nonprofits; neighbors; faculty members in schools and colleges; and associates and colleagues of all kinds. Mediation is an extremely rewarding process because we have seen tangible results of people arriving at agreements of their own making.

Although our clients have often sat down at the mediation table "breathing fire" at each other, in more than 90 percent of the cases we have mediated, they have resolved their issues and ended up hugging each other—or at least shaking hands.

Even so, we developed a gnawing concern that we hadn't been as helpful to our clients as we might have been. We always wished them well, but as they left the mediation room with copies of signed agreements, we privately questioned whether they had learned all the skills they needed to handle future conflicts on their own.

We decided to do something about that!

We developed a curriculum based on the structured communication principles that are the foundation of the mediation process. We then used the curriculum to teach conflict-resolution skills to a broad spectrum of classroom students and workshop participants. They have ranged from middle-school children to public- and private-school teachers and college professors; from city council members to boards of directors. Our client list has included employees and volunteers in public and private organizations of all kinds.

Our curriculum became the basis of this book. The Learn2Resolve method for resolving interpersonal conflicts emphasizes the need for individuals to develop certain skills: understanding how our minds work; practicing self-awareness; listening for understanding; identifying our own assumptions and those we make about others; clarifying and validating these assumptions with one another; and ultimately reaching agreement on a fresh path forward.

This works well in a structured setting, but in daily life, it's not as easy. People seldom reflect on their thoughts and feelings about the people they're butting heads with. They rarely open up to receive the thoughts and feelings of the people they're fighting with. And rarely do they engage in a dialogue that allows the feuding parties to discuss their assumptions about each other and work together to determine which are valid and which aren't.

This is the domain of *Conflict—The Unexpected Gift*. We are presenting it as a handbook you can use to acquire the skills to span impasses and repair broken relationships. We explain why conflicts at first seem so intractable; why people often falter when trying to resolve their issues; and why people sometimes avoid conflicts altogether.

This book is intended to help people of all ages develop conflict-resolution skills. Each chapter offers concrete steps for learning a new way to communicate that helps resolve conflicts and builds more viable relationships with family members, friends, acquaintances, and other people with whom we interact. The real-life vignettes included in each chapter show how others have handled conflict.

How to Use This Book

It can be challenging to take the steps necessary to resolve conflicts. Personal relationships are complicated. Empathy, for example, is a skill we believe is a necessary building block to help resolve conflicts. Yet, it is a struggle to step away from a conditioned way of looking at things from only your own perspective. You might not really believe you can step into someone else's shoes. We'll show you how you can. You'll find exercises you can use to enhance your empathy skills. Our own professional experiences indicate the methods we prescribe are effective. We've seen them change people's lives.

This book was designed for you to be able to read the chapters in any order, so you can quickly access information pertinent to your particular situation. However, we strongly suggest you start by reading chapter 1, "The Ladder of Assumptions," because the Ladder plays a central role in the book. In order to be even-handed in the use of genders, we have used the feminine and masculine pronouns interchangeably, when writing in general terms.

This book will help you recognize that the behavior of others has very little to do with you. A person's behavior toward you may be caused by a number of factors, including many the person isn't even aware of. A person's behavior is often the result of things happening in *that* person's life at *that* time. Other contributing factors are heredity, early life conditioning, cultural factors, traumatic experiences, and even basic needs that have not been adequately met. (How receptive are you to resolving a problem when you've been up all night?)

Something you did or said may have been a trigger for another person's reactions, but you neither caused that person's behavior nor were responsible for it. Her actions might have been directed toward you because you happened to be the closest or easiest person to unleash her pent-up emotions on. Maybe your mere presence and proximity was enough to prompt her action. It didn't have to be directed at you; you just happened to have been there to receive it.

Conflict—The Unexpected Gift is replete with anecdotes and cases from our work with various clients, students, and workshop participants, as well as from our own lives. To ensure confidentiality, we have changed all identifying facts.

It is our firm conviction that a set of practices designed and intended to help people become more skillful at resolving conflicts is one way we can nudge the world—one strengthened relationship at a time—toward solving the growing number of problems that result from breakdowns in interpersonal relationships. When people learn to communicate in this way, there will eventually be fewer misunderstandings, less violence, and decreased outbreaks of war.

Conflict is an unexpected gift—an opportunity for change. A pearl starts as an irritation in an oyster. Similarly, a conflict can lead to a new awareness and a new openness in your relationships. Resolving interpersonal conflicts is a process. In the course of analyzing your conflict, you learn to let go of unfounded assumptions and pave new chapters in your relationships. A conflict, when reconciled, can be the gift of a second chance.

CHAPTER 1

THE LADDER OF ASSUMPTIONS

The least questioned assumptions are
often the most questionable.

—Paul Broca

An executive at a nonprofit association was getting increasingly frustrated with a woman who reported to her. The executive felt the woman wasn't a team player. She wasn't doing her work quickly, and the executive felt sure the employee was just coming to work to draw a paycheck without feeling any commitment to the organization.

We talked to the executive (whose story we'll delve into in more detail) when she participated in a workshop we conducted at her organization. As we helped her pinpoint the cause of her frustration with her employee, she recognized she had made assumptions about her employee that were not true. Those assumptions were threatening to rupture the organization.

Most of us experience this feeling of helplessness, often in the form of frustration, on a daily basis. The interpersonal issues we face can be as small as deciding which family member gets to sit in the front passenger seat of the car or as complex as figuring out how to restore professional relations with a former coworker you now manage. They can be as life changing as one spouse wanting children and the other wishing to remain childless. And they can be as mundane as one teammate stewing over another teammate's not pulling his weight.

Even the most ordinary interpersonal challenge can leave you frozen and incapable of figuring out your next step. What on earth can you do when there is no obvious way for one of you to "win" the dispute without the other person "losing"?

A key to resolving interpersonal conflicts involves understanding how the human mind works. People tend to make negative judgments based on their assumptions about who caused a conflict in which they're involved. So a person caught up in conflict often will blame the other individual for having caused the dispute or will try to put pieces together that don't always lead to a correct whole. That may ease anxieties for a time, but it doesn't ultimately resolve the conflict in a way that leaves both people satisfied.

To truly reach an accord after a disagreement, you need to become more aware of what actually motivates you and your partner in conflict, rather than what your conditioned way of thinking leads you to believe.

How Does Your Mind Make Sense of the World?

Consider the human brain as a sort of finely tuned computer designed to make quick, survival-oriented decisions based on input from the environment. Understanding people would be an overwhelming process if we had to start from scratch with every human contact. We all are exposed to more input from the world than we can possibly manage. Instead, we classify the infinite variety of human beings into workable groups of types. These generalized images help us define people so we can readily understand them.

In effect, the categories we create and use determine the assumptions we make about people. Those assumptions affect our understanding of them as well as our relationships with them. For example, for hundreds—if not thousands—of years, people with mental illnesses have been stereotyped as "crazy" people, "kooks," or at the very least "lazy" individuals who could overcome their mental problems if they only tried hard enough.

However, in recent years, scientists have discovered that many mental illnesses, including schizophrenia, are caused by biologically based brain disorders rather than by lack of effort or interest on the part of an individual. People with such illnesses can now be more or less effectively treated with drugs and psychotherapy. With such scientific and clinical data available, we have to change our assumptions. We must remove the stereotypes of the past and view mentally ill people as ordinary people who happen to have illnesses.

From our earliest years, when we first begin to typecast people, we see others in terms of our standardized pictures. For good or bad, our parents and guardians and our earliest teachers help us form those categories.

In the musical *South Pacific*, which deals with racial prejudice, composers Richard Rodgers and Oscar Hammerstein II outline this widespread learning process in the song "You've Got to Be Carefully Taught."[1]

> *You've got to be taught to hate and fear,*
> *You've got to be taught from year to year,*
> *It's got to be drummed in your dear little ear.*
> *You've got to be carefully taught!*
>
> *You've got to be taught to be afraid*
> *Of people whose eyes are oddly made,*
> *And people whose skin is a different shade,*
> *You've got to be carefully taught.*
>
> *You've got to be taught before it's too late,*
> *Before you are six or seven or eight,*
> *To hate all the people your relatives hate,*
> *You've got to be carefully taught!*
> *You've got to be carefully taught!*

---

1   Oscar Hammerstein II and Richard Rodgers, "You've Got to Be Carefully Taught," *South Pacific*, ©1949.

The song deals with the issue of xenophobia and the societal conditioning that leads to fearing people who are superficially different from us. The message of the lyrics is that prejudice is learned—something that is "carefully taught" to children by parents or society.

It may be extremely difficult to ever achieve a prejudice-free society because of the way our minds function. Even in racially homogeneous societies, people develop prejudices over other differences, such as gender, sexual orientation, birthplace, or religion. You see this when professionals whose lives depend on quick decisions regarding human behavior, such as police officers and military personnel, are trained to process information carefully and swiftly in doing their jobs.

But even ordinary citizens, without training or practice, make instant decisions on the basis of scant information to differentiate between friend and foe. They often do this in situations that are not life threatening and that, in many cases, lead to conflict. So how do you avoid this behavior? In our work and studies, we have found that people can help eliminate hasty and flawed generalizations that contribute to clashes in two important ways:

1. by becoming aware of those situations in which they make instantaneous judgments based on preconceived categorizations and

2. by taking the time necessary to resolve a conflict using open-minded, nonjudgmental methods.

The Use and Abuse of Stereotypes

Do you know someone who makes a quick judgment and then has a hard time changing his mind? That seems to be human nature. What makes these judgments hard to change is that they are often completely unconscious. They are the result of the system of generalized categories people have developed. We quickly refer to this system when we receive new information. Generalizations that are not consistent with current facts become stereotypes and lead to breakdowns in communication. To stop the stereotypes, we have to process new information and allow that information to update our personal categories. But doing so requires reflection, openness, and patience. And that takes time.

Stereotypes may be based on a kernel of truth, but they go beyond the facts at hand. They depend on sweeping claims that usually have little or no basis, leaving us with nothing more than a set of unfounded assumptions. No tools. No ideas. Just unfounded assumptions.

San Franciscan Tony Jonick experienced firsthand what it meant to be prejudged when, wearing a long, scraggly beard and haircut for an acting role, he found himself being treated differently than he was used to being treated. He described what happened in a "perspective" piece he contributed to public radio station KQED-FM. Here's an excerpt:[2]

> Last week, after working out in the gym, I realized I'd left my work-shirt at home and was stuck wearing the tank top I'd been exercising in. Between that stinking shirt and my ratty jacket, I was … "a homeless man" wandering into a safe suburban space. Faces turned toward me, and noses wrinkled in the coffee shop. As I wandered the supermarket aisles deciding on lunch, there was always an eye on me. Finally, I stopped at a store to buy a shirt, and people put their heads together and whispered when I tried one on. When I made my purchase by credit card, my driver's license was closely scrutinized.

> In today's modern jungle, we crowded apes try to make a thousand judgments about those around us. We use our evolved primate skill of facial recognition, constantly scanning for people we know, people out of place, and people who are threats. If no danger is perceived, we scan and move on. With a clean shirt and a trim, I'm just one more face in the mass of uninteresting

2   Tony Jonick, "My Day as a Threat," *Perspectives* (San Francisco: KQED-FM, Feb. 19, 2008).

monkeys. But I was shocked at how quickly I could become the threat.

I can only imagine the frustration of people who are misjudged at every turn—because of clothes, color, culture. I only touched the merest edge of what some people deal with every day, when our snap judgments give us the wrong signal, and we misjudge ordinary people as dangerous. Can I see past a person's shell and into his or her heart with a glance? Of course not. But I do hope I will pause and think twice before the alarm bells arbitrarily go off in my ape brain. I'd like to live with less fear and suspicion in my life.

Jonick's experience demonstrates how stereotypes cause us to base a judgment about a person on a limited amount of evidence, as if that represented everything about the person. We're constantly reliving stereotypes acquired from our past experiences in the present. Our present perceptions are so influenced by the past that we are usually unable to see the immediate happenings in our lives without distortions.

Stereotypes Become Substitutes for Careful Observation

Most of us don't remember where our most deeply embedded assumptions came from. The situations that gave rise to these stereotypes were forgotten long ago. Eventually, we come to think of our longstanding assumptions as facts. But, unknown to us, we're several steps removed from the facts.

People who have formed rigid preconceptions often find it difficult to alter their point of view when meeting someone who doesn't fit the mold. In the following story, high school student Andrew, who as an eighth grader participated in our class on conflict resolution, tells how frustrating it was for him when his friends could not see him as the person he believed he truly was.

Andrew Is Stereotyped

"You're an Oreo! Black on the outside and white on the inside!" I've heard these words over and over again from some of my peers. They've labeled me as "whitewashed." I've developed a thick skin in response to their name calling. But it still bothers me that among my peers race plays such a large role in our society, even though hateful racism is not intended.

As an African American living in a predominantly Caucasian community, I feel like I've been the diversity poster child my entire life. I find it ironic that my peers see me as fitting a stereotype rather than as a

9

lifelong member of my community whose values match theirs. I definitely do not fit the mold of the typical black stereotype portrayed by our society.

Working around racial stereotypes has proven to be one of the most powerful life lessons I've encountered. To gain acceptance as a young kid, I changed my mannerisms when I was with my African American friends. As I grew up, I realized my different behavior in various social circles only perpetuated the stereotypes. By not being true to myself, I wasn't being a true friend, and I was not appreciated for who I really was.

Now, all my friends, regardless of race or background, know my true personality. What I once described as being stuck between two worlds has actually afforded me opportunities to be trusted by people from multiple cultures. I feel I've worked hard to dissipate any covert stereotypes that may still remain.

My life straddles two cultures. I've learned to embrace both, just as my forefathers did.

Andrew's account reveals how difficult it is for people to change their perceptions of stereotypes. It also shows the negative impact stereotypes have on the person who doesn't fit the label he's been branded with.

Judging and Being Misjudged

People in the throes of a disagreement often fling the accusation, "You can't read my mind!" at their opponent. Yet most of us do feel we can read others' minds. We subconsciously place people into the categories we carefully craft. But those uniquely designed categories may be unreasonable or dated. And then our behavior is off-kilter because we based our assumptions on the other person being a member of a certain category in which she's not a member. She is likely to feel misjudged, leading to possible conflict.

If we feel other people are making incorrect judgments about us, we become confused, angry, or feel diminished. We feel insulted by the other person, even though that person's words may have nothing to do with us personally. The opinions they express flow from their own life experiences.

When you take things personally, it is only natural for you to feel offended, hurt, or angry. And once you feel offended, it is human nature for you to want to defend your actions. That can lead to conflicts.

The Ladder of Assumptions

To overcome the predicaments caused by conflicts in our lives, we need to first understand that when we respond to a situation involving conflict, most of us quickly and unconsciously climb something we call a "Ladder of Assumptions." It's a useful metaphor for how the mind works, and it draws on the work of Chris Argyris.

The Ladder allows you to analyze conflicts by establishing the setting for the conflicts and the actions you take as a result of the conflicts. The rungs of the Ladder are the elements of the conflicts. Say you are a sports-car driver speeding and weaving in and out of lanes on a highway. This is how the Ladder would work:

Setting. At any given moment, the feet of our mental Ladder are set in a particular situation. Included in this setting is all observable, verifiable information in a situation— information that could be captured electronically by, say, a video recorder. The setting includes the physical space from every conceivable angle.

Actions

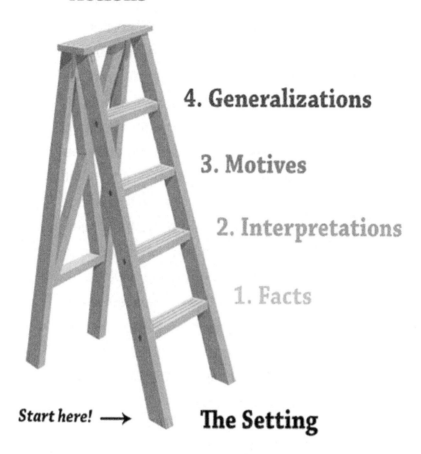

4. **Generalizations**

3. **Motives**

2. **Interpretations**

1. Facts

Start here! ⟶ **The Setting**

As you race along the highway, the setting is the road. There may be trees lining the sides of the road, a median in the middle, several signs along the way, and other cars. Our minds are not capable of taking in the entire setting of situations. For example, as you're driving along, you may not have seen a police car on the side of the road. **Key: There is more to a setting than what we experience.**

Rung 1: Facts. A fact is a piece of reality known by actual experience or observation. The facts we observe are the portion of the setting, or reality, that we are able to take in. No matter how skilled we are at observing, we can take in only a subset of the total facts of any situation. Your position in a situation—and your past experiences in similar situations—significantly limit what you are able to take in. The first incorrect assumption we make is that we have seen the whole picture and that what we have seen is also what other people have seen. One fact (of many) in this example setting is this: "That driver is driving twenty miles per hour over the speed limit and is changing lanes without signaling." **Key: A fact can be experienced or observed.**

Rung 2: Interpretations. We interpret the facts we perceive. Conflicts often come about when we confuse our interpretations with facts that can be objectively verified. Our "interpretations" should really be defined as "opinions." We make interpretations to make sense out of the sliver of facts that we have perceived. We often interpret a current situation based on our personal history. Consider if someone watching you speed along the highway comments, "There goes another crazy sports-car driver." ***Key: When you use adjectives to describe a person's behavior or a particular situation, you're generally making an interpretation.***

Rung 3: Motives. We tend to attribute ulterior motives to the other person who has annoyed or offended us with his or her behavior. "He just wanted to—"; "She thinks—." We can't really know what another person is thinking, but we often think we can. What we attribute to the other person's behavior is typically based on our own experiences in similar situations that have long-since slipped under the radar of our awareness. A thought such as, *That driver thinks he's the king of the road and doesn't care if he causes havoc on the highway* is one that attributes a motive to the observed driver. ***Key: When you assign a feeling, emotion, or some other word implying an intention to your description of how a person is behaving, you are attributing a motive to that person.***

Rung 4: Generalizations. We invoke generalizations based on our interpretations of the limited facts we have perceived— and on our confidence in our mind-reading abilities. Generalizations are the thoughts we carry in our subconscious minds about categories of objects, events, or groups of people. We generalize to make sense out of our complicated world, but this can create a slippery slope to stereotyping and prejudice. A stereotype or prejudice is an oversimplified generalization where individuals are typecast with certain characteristics because of their real or perceived membership in a particular group.

When we observe the particular behavior of an individual, our minds will quickly squeeze that behavior into a category, whether it fits or not. For example, someone watching you race might mutter, "That driver is just like all other sports-car drivers. They're all power hungry and want to show off. They don't think they have to follow the same rules we do. They're always causing accidents." ***Key: Using plural pronouns, such as "they" or "them," and category descriptions such as "all" to describe a behavior, indicates you have assigned a person to a predetermined category.***

Actions. We are usually aware of our actions but quite unaware of the reflexive, "knee-jerk" mental process that took us up the Ladder and got us to those actions. For example, someone might think, *That driver's a danger to everyone on the road. He deserves to learn a little lesson. If he cuts in front of me, I'm not letting him get away with it. I'm going to pass him and do the same thing back. Someone has to show him he's just wrong.* A driver does something (a fact). Another person reacts (based on an assumption, correct or incorrect) and retaliates (action). That is "racing up the Ladder."

Sometimes a person acts in a particular setting by simply selecting certain facts and assuming those are the only facts in the situation (Rung No. 1), or by simply making an interpretation of the facts he perceives (Rung No. 2) and doesn't necessarily attribute motives to individuals (Rung No. 3), or label people with stereotypes (Rung No. 4).

A Triple A Traffic Safety Foundation study found that many cases of what we call "road rage" are caused by "simple misunderstandings between drivers."[3] Yet the response to such mix-ups, which may have begun with assumptions that led to anger, can result in physical aggression, according to Matthew Joint, head of behavioral analysis for the foundation.[4] **Key: When you act, you might not**

---

3   Matthew Joint, "Road Rage" for the Automobile Association Group Public Policy Road Safety Unit, AAA Foundation for Traffic Safety, Washington, DC: March 1995, accessed Feb. 16, 2012, http://www.aaafoundation.org/resources/index.cfm?button=agdrtext#Road%20Rage.

4   Ibid.

even realize the assumptions you made that led to your actions.

Acknowledging the Origin of Conflicts

Becoming conscious of the mental process by which we reach conclusions about others gives us the power to make changes. We can use the Ladder of Assumptions as a tool to help us reach a more valid understanding of who others really are and what actually motivates them, rather than what our ingrained mental patterns often lead us to believe. We can ask clarifying questions of others to find out whether our assumptions about their behavior are correct, and we can let go of erroneous assumptions when we find out what the people have actually been observing and thinking. In this way, interactions with others can become less conflicted and more positive.

Carlos Lozada, an economic analyst in Atlanta, captured the essence of this goal in a column in *The Christian Science Monitor* a number of years ago. He said he dreamed of a day when people would eventually become open to the possibility that they can view Latinos as varied as people of any other group and that people would see him primarily as an economist who just happens to be Latino. He wrote, "I don't wish to live in a world in which my skin tone becomes my single, all-important attribute, and I would be offended if, based on my racial background, someone extrapolated assumptions about my beliefs, intelligence, or customs."[5]

Now that you understand the basics of the Ladder of Assumptions, let's explore how to use it to defuse the volatile elements of a conflict.

Myra and Her Staff Member

Remember the executive at the nonprofit who had reached an impasse with an employee? During one of our workshops, she used the Ladder to examine her perceptions of the situation. Here's how the executive, whom we shall call Myra, described the conflict:

> I was upset with Sandy's performance. When I finally was able to take a deep breath, I identified all the rungs of a Ladder of Assumptions I had climbed:
>
> - The **setting** was the building in which both of us worked.
>
> - The **facts** were that I am a manager of a team, while Sandy is a member of that team who performs work tasks for the team.
>
> - I **interpreted** Sandy as a plodder who

---

5   Carlos Lozada, "Politically Correct, Linguistically Out-to-Lunch," *The Christian Science Monitor*, July 16, 1998, 16.

takes forever to complete an assignment and thus drags down the overall performance of the team.

- The **motive** I attributed to her was that she was concerned only about getting a regular salary and didn't care about how well the team functioned.

- I **stereotyped** her as one of those union members who do as little as they can to still keep their jobs.

- My **actions** were that I got very angry at her.

I had quickly "climbed" my Ladder, and I stayed at the top for two days before analyzing what happened. After I went through my Ladder of Assumptions, I arranged to meet with Sandy. The meeting helped me go back down my Ladder rung by rung and acknowledge where my assumptions about Sandy were not realistic. We were able to talk about our different approaches to "getting a job done." We agreed I tend to be quick out of the starting gates and am more of a risk taker, while she is more methodical and detail-oriented. By talking about it, we both realized each of us brings distinct skills to our work setting that benefit the entire department. That discussion helped us get off to a fresh start and establish a much better working relationship.

Myra told us the Ladder of Assumptions changed the way she dealt with disputes. "I had always felt that if I needed to deal with conflict I was having with another person, I would do it directly and openly by confronting the person with what he or she was doing wrong." Going rung by rung through the Ladder helped Myra analyze her own actions and deal with the problem "internally":

> I discovered that when conflict occurs, if you do not deal with it internally and figure out what is occurring at the time—or as quickly as you can collect yourself to do so—the conflict will occur over and over again.
>
> Since learning about the Ladder of Assumptions, I've begun to internalize the Ladder's rungs. It's helped me realize where my responsibility starts in a conflict and how to prevent that conflict from escalating. Now, when a knot starts getting tight in my stomach, I try to ask myself, "Where am I on the Ladder, and what do I need to do to climb back down?"

Myra applied the lesson she had learned earlier and took

the lead in resolving the conflict with Sandy. It turned the relationship around and made all the difference in her work environment. Myra's Ladder and her conversation with Sandy were the first steps in building resolution. She acknowledged that the frustration she had been experiencing was largely based on assumptions she'd made that weren't rooted in reality. Once she recognized that, she and her organization could move on.

Practicing Probing to Defuse Anger

If you find yourself angry with someone, you can help defuse your anger if you remember that you may have made incorrect assumptions about that person. To help move away from the anger, frustration, and hurt, you need to learn how to act differently. Anger, frustration, and hurt are negative, inward-facing emotions that can cloud the path to open dialogue. Just as you train muscle groups for a sport, you need to train your mind to take a more positive approach to difficult interpersonal situations. Your first goal should be to determine the basis for your assumptions and those of others by discussing with them the validity of your respective assumptions.

Concluding Tips

Focus on your mind being filled with unconscious assumptions that can cause you to instantly judge the behavior of others. This can ignite conflict. These simple steps can help you retrain your mind:

1. Acknowledge you have preformed opinions about people. When you are receiving new information, be aware of opinions you have already formed and try to put them aside.

2. Commit to looking within and examining where those opinions originated. Consider the people in your background who have had a major influence on the way you think.

3. Be diligent every day in observing how you react to people. Look at interactions you have with another person as an opportunity to learn more about how your mind works.

Maintain an open mind about others.

1. Be willing to entertain the possibility that people don't always fit the categories in which your mind has placed them. Give yourself permission to change your mindset about people.

2. Allow yourself to imagine other dimensions to a situation than your first reaction. Consider that your first reaction can be incorrect.

3. When you think you understand the intent behind a person's behavior, imagine a different explanation. Know that your original reasoning about the motive for a person's behavior is based on *your* life

experience, which is usually quite different from that of the person.

Activities

Give yourself a minute or two to look at the phrase below and count the number of occurrences of the letter F; if possible, ask two others to do the same.

FEATURE FILMS ARE THE RESULT

OF YEARS OF SCIENTIFIC

STUDY COMBINED WITH

THE EXPERIENCE OF YEARS.

How many Fs did you count? Did the three of you agree on the number of Fs in the phrase? We present this exercise to groups of approximately twenty people, and there is never agreement. This activity often provides an amusing lesson in humility about how we often can't even agree on the facts—the first rung on the Ladder of Assumptions. You've all seen the exact same phrase; you should all be able to agree on how many times the letter F appears. (The answer, by the way, is six.)

The "I Search" exercise

This exercise should be written in three sections:

1. What I assume to be true about someone
2. The Interview
3. What I learned

Here's what you do:

1. **What I assume to be true about someone.** Write a Ladder of Assumptions that exists in your mind about someone with whom you have had a recent experience, not necessarily a conflict.

2. **The Interview.** Schedule time to talk with the person with whom you have had a recent experience. Ask her if you can share the Ladder of Assumptions you wrote about her, in the light of that experience. If she is willing to allow you to do that, discuss how accurate your assumptions seem to be and write down the comments she makes.

3. **What I learned.** After concluding your interview, compare your Ladder of Assumptions with the comments made by the person you interviewed. Write what you learned about the accuracy of the assumptions you made about her.

CHAPTER 2

SELF-AWARENESS

If one is out of touch with oneself,
then one cannot touch others.

—Anne Morrow Lindbergh

Very often, the Ladder of Assumptions exposes your own deeply rooted beliefs. One of us met Natasha when she was a freshman having trouble fitting in with her peers at a San Francisco Bay Area university. Newly arrived from Ukraine, Natasha found herself shrinking back from interactions with fellow students. One voice in her head told her to get to know these intelligent people with interesting ideas. The other warned her that to do so would open herself to the risk of being taken advantage of. It was a confusing time for her.

To end the confusion, Natasha had to delve deep within to discover the roots of her inhibitions and become more aware of herself. You will read about her discovery process later in this chapter.

Finding Humility

Developing self-awareness is basic to psychological health. You need to learn to catch your mind in the moment, especially when *you* are rushing to judgment. It builds your capacity to observe your thoughts and feelings without necessarily acting on them. When you recognize—as you read in chapter 1—just how inaccurately your mind can function in the moment before you take action, your level of humility rises.

We need to be humble enough to acknowledge that however we interpret someone else's behavior—however we judge a situation—it is only from one point of view: our own. And that is only one of many possible perspectives. It is our own particular collection of subjective thoughts. Whenever we rush to judgment, we need to face the fact that we could very well be wrong.

Here are stories of three people who used their self-reflection skills to recognize they had caused conflicts with others by racing up the Ladders of Assumptions they created about the other parties. These individuals used the same self-reflection skills to resolve those conflicts by going back down their Ladders to the "rung of facts" and checking the validity of the assumptions they had made.

Kathy Catches Herself in the Moment

Kathy and Eileen, two volunteer members of a standing committee of a community association, had a conflict. The conflict erupted at a meeting of the committee. Here's how the conflict played out:

> **Kathy**: When it's time to contact members about renewing their memberships, an online registration and payment system will make things so much simpler. Our manager can just send an e-mail to members to tell them it's time to go to the association website and renew their memberships. This will save the manager and the volunteers a lot of time. It'll be much more efficient than delivering or mailing packets to members. As we all know, some of those packets get lost in the shuffle and are never opened by our members. Also, sending e-mails will be good for the environment because it saves a lot of paper.

> **Eileen**: I'm sorry, Kathy, but your idea won't work at all. The e-mail will just end up in people's spam filters. So it'll be even less efficient than our regular way of contacting members about renewing. I know what I'm talking about. I send out a lot of e-mails in my business, and many never reach the

intended recipients. It's really frustrating sending e-mail blasts that never get to prospective clients.

Kathy: Eileen, you're being so negative.

Eileen didn't respond to Kathy's statement. The committee members continued with their discussion, without anyone responding to Kathy's or Eileen's comments. Several days later, we conducted a mediation between Kathy and Eileen. Before the session, we had asked Kathy to write a Ladder of Assumptions she had raced up regarding Eileen and asked Eileen to write a Ladder of Assumptions she had raced up about Kathy.

Here is what Kathy wrote:

- The **setting** was the living room of a house in the neighborhood.

- The **facts** were that the community association membership committee members were discussing different ways member fees could be collected more efficiently.

- I **interpreted** Eileen's response to my suggestion as abrupt, dismissive, and condescending.

- The **motive** I attributed to Eileen was that she wanted to show the committee members that she had much more expertise in the matter than I did.

- I **stereotyped** her as one of those female professionals who acts as if she knows it all but is actually insecure.

- My **actions** were to get angry and accuse Eileen of being unreasonably negative.

Kathy and Eileen each brought copies of their Ladders of Assumptions to the mediation table and shared them with each other during the course of the mediation. Following that dialogue, Kathy spoke about the exchange between her and Eileen that had taken place at the committee meeting:

> **Kathy**: Eileen, I want to say I'm sorry I jumped on you at the committee meeting and criticized you for being so negative. I know I do that to my kids sometimes, and I'm working on not doing it.
>
> **Eileen** (with a serious look on her face): Yes, you did jump on me, Kathy!
>
> **Kathy**: Well, I'm working on my awareness, and I know what I did was wrong. I'm truly sorry, Eileen.
>
> **Eileen** (with a smile on her face): I accept your apology.

Even though Eileen had made abrupt remarks during the

committee meeting, Kathy took responsibility for her own reaction to them. Kathy recognized she had raced up a Ladder of Assumptions and concluded that Eileen had tried to put her down. This insight about herself enabled her to go back down her Ladder to the rung of facts and take responsibility for the incorrect assumptions she had made about Eileen and for the angry response she had made to her. Kathy's flash of self-awareness and humility opened a door to resolving the tension between her and Eileen.

Sarah Gets Angry at One of Her Students

Consider the story of Sarah, a forty-four-year old woman who teaches at a junior high school. She contacted one of us for help in resolving a conflict she had with one of her students. She applied the approach described in this book to deal constructively with her feelings. Here is her description of what happened:

> It was the last week of the spring semester. The previous day, my students had had a substitute teacher because I had been ill. I stood in the doorway of my classroom and greeted the students as they entered. I felt very good about my students and believed I had established a good rapport with them. I had worked hard all year long teaching them, and I believed they appreciated the efforts I had made. I tried a little joke with one of

the boys as he walked through the doorway. I said, "Would you rather have me or a sub as your teacher today?" I absolutely could not believe it when he said, "A sub! A sub!" What he said really hurt me deeply.

Here is the Ladder of Assumptions about the student I had created in my mind:

- The **setting** was a seventh-grade social studies classroom at a junior high school.

- The **facts** were that I stood at the door of my classroom at the beginning of one of my classes and spoke to the students as they entered. I asked a boy, "Would you rather have me or a sub today?" He said, "A sub. A sub."

- I **interpreted** his behavior as disrespectful, hurtful and cruel.

- The **motive** I attributed to him was that on one of the last days of the school year, he wanted to joke around with his friends in the classroom. He knew he could do that with a sub but that I wouldn't permit it.

- I **stereotyped** him as one of those

thirteen-year-old boys who often say mean things.

- My **actions** were that I felt hurt that all the hard work I had put into teaching the class that year had been a waste of time. I cried in front of the class and told my students I felt I had been disrespected.

After school that day, I went home and cried all night. I felt defeated as a teacher, a profession in which I had devoted seventeen years of my life. The next day, I decided I would quit my career as a teacher and not return to the school the next year. I felt totally relieved and at peace after making that decision.

Over the next several days, I had long talks with my husband, my father, and some of my closest friends. The more I talked with them, the more I realized I had made the decision to quit teaching while I was feeling low and while I was struggling with the emotional effects of having taken the boy's words personally. I thought about the Ladder of Assumptions I had created in my mind about what the boy had said to me. I tried hard to go back down my Ladder to the factual rung and then figure out how wrong I had been with my assumptions.

I acknowledged I had taken the boy's comments personally when they actually had nothing to do with me. I realized that during the last few days of the school year, he no doubt was eager to get away from school for the summer and simply wanted to have fun in my classroom. The comments were made by a boy who was tired of school, not by a boy who was trying to be disrespectful to me. Reflecting on all this, I took a deep breath, slowly exhaled, and finally decided to continue as a teacher at my school.

Sarah went through a heartfelt process of reflection. She looked within and identified all the hurt and anger she had felt toward her student that had resulted from her Ladder of Assumptions. She took responsibility for her assumptions and acknowledged they probably were not based in reality and that she had taken his comments personally. In the end, she saw that her decision to quit her teaching career had been impulsive. This gave her the inner peace to reverse her decision to quit her profession and continue with her teaching.

Natasha's Growth in Self-Awareness

We discussed the Ladder of Assumptions with Natasha, the freshman student newly arrived from her home country of Ukraine. She used it to reflect on something disturbing she had learned in childhood:

> When I was twenty years old, I left Ukraine for the United States to attend an American college. I especially remember the advice my mother gave me before I left. She told me not to develop close relationships with Jews or men of dark skin color. I can't say I was shocked by my mother's statements because my family members, as well as most Ukrainian people, tend to avoid relationships with people who are different from us.
>
> Since early childhood, my parents had told me to be very careful around Jews because my parents believed them to be selfish, sly, and greedy. My parents told me Jews used whatever means necessary to achieve their own goals and that Jews strove to be prosperous regardless of the price others had to pay for their success. This suspicion and outright dislike of Jewish people was not peculiar to my family but, rather, was widely accepted by the majority of Ukrainian people.

In Ukraine, stereotypes also persist about people who have dark skin color—stereotypes that may have gotten started in the 1960s, when thousands of African students came to Soviet universities to study. These students were among the first large groups of Africans many Ukrainians had ever experienced face-to-face. Ukrainians viewed them as foreigners who came from strange countries and who carried rare diseases with them.

Unaccustomed to the Ukrainian custom of not speaking to strangers on the street, African male students were viewed as crude and vulgar when they approached Ukrainians whom they didn't know and spoke to them in loud voices. When Ukrainian girls or women were singled out for social overtures by African male students, the men were labeled as black warriors who could not control their sex drives.

Once, when I was a little girl, my mother took me to a restaurant for dinner. At the restaurant, we had to wait in line behind some students from Africa. It was the first time I had observed these different people so closely. They talked to each other in a language unknown to me. I looked at their hands and compared them to mine. I was stunned by the contrast. I recall that I was too scared to look at their faces.

My mother left me alone for a few minutes. After she left, one of the African men turned around, greeted me in flawed Russian, and patted me on the back. I did not take time to think about what had happened. All I remember are the feelings of surprise, fear, and anger that rose up in me. I ran away from the line and found my mother. I was still shaking when I told my mother about the stranger's gesture.

Even though I'm now much older and living in the United States, I still seem to carry around those same stereotypes. I'm still quite apprehensive toward people who seem to fit those stereotypes. I decided I needed to write my Ladder of Assumptions about these people. Here is what I wrote.

- The **setting** was my hometown in Kiev, Ukraine.

- The **facts** were that my mother told me to have nothing to do with Jews and with men with dark complexions.

- I adopted my mother's **interpretations** that Jews were sly, greedy, and ruthless and that men of dark skin color were crude, vulgar, and unhealthy and were sexual maniacs.

- The **motives** my mother attributed to Jews and men of dark skin color, which I accepted, were that Jews would not let anything stand in their way of achieving economic success and that men with dark skin color were driven to take advantage of women sexually.

- Just as my mother did, I **stereotyped** Jews as a group of religious fanatics desirous of attaining wealth at any price and men with dark skin color as a racial class with subhuman characteristics.

- My **actions**, like those of my mother, were to fear Jews and men with dark skin color and to avoid them whenever possible.

I'm struggling to accept that I have prejudiced attitudes, even though it wasn't a matter of choice but picked up from the prejudice radiating from the people around me while I was growing up in Ukraine. I'm hopeful I can reverse the process by going back down my Ladder of Assumptions and unlearn these assumptions and prejudices. I keep reminding myself that if they were taught to me when I was young, I ought to be able to teach myself to give them up and replace them with attitudes that are based on facts rather than fears.

It's a lot of hard work to open my mind and lift the veil of my stereotypes. But I want to be able to get to know better individuals who look, act, and talk differently than I do. So my goal is to try to communicate with them and understand them. If I don't do these things, I realize I'll always fear people who appear different than I am.

Natasha has reached a level of self-awareness that has enabled her to understand how stereotypes learned in childhood prevent her from getting to know her fellow students as individuals rather than as representatives of stereotypes that have little or no basis in fact.

Natasha realized that without a sincere effort on her part to break down these stereotypes, her behavior would continue to be driven by fear rather than by a willingness to enrich her life by developing relationships with students who are different from her.

How to Practice Self-Awareness

Dedicating time to practice self-awareness through self-reflection requires substantial effort in highly scheduled cultures. Practicing self-reflection is like practicing a sport or a musical instrument. The objective of practice is to internalize new behaviors. The more regularly you give yourself the gift of time to practice self-reflection, the easier it will become to remember to be fully aware and present in the moment when experiencing and working toward resolution of interpersonal conflicts.

Start your day by quietly reminding yourself to participate fully in positive conflict-resolution behaviors. Try thinking about each of the following statements as a way to prepare yourself to be present for the entire day:

- I anticipate that opportunities to practice conflict resolution will arise today.

- I will work toward perceiving these opportunities when they arise.

- I will be open to using the opportunities presented to further my practice of conflict resolution.

- I will try to respond to conflicts creatively and positively.

- I hope to learn from my efforts to resolve conflicts.

- I will be grateful for the opportunities to further my own learning process and reach creative resolutions.

At the end of your day, set aside a few minutes to reflect on how your day has gone. Some examples of how to reflect include the following:

- writing in a journal or writing a blog
- drawing
- developing a computer graphic
- composing music
- meditating

Challenge yourself to bring to the surface assumptions you formed in the past so you can determine what effect they are having on your behavior in the current moment. Bring your assumptions to the surface, become aware of their origins, and determine their relevance in current situations. Avoid living on the basis of unfounded assumptions you have formed over time. By taking the time to examine your own thoughts, you will find it is less likely for you to spread stereotypes.

Concluding Tips

Observe your behavior toward others in the moment and check it out.

1. Identify another person's behavior that is

objectionable to you. Acknowledge that you typically blame the other person for your reactions.

2. Own your emotions when you find yourself reacting to someone. The reactions you are having to that person are your own; no one else is causing them.

3. Describe how you are acting when you react to someone. Identify the emotions you're having that seem to be causing you to act this way.

Try to figure out why your mind rushes to judgment about others.

1. Bring to the surface feelings, positive or negative, that you have toward others. Identify the thoughts that trigger the feelings.

2. Notice any preconceptions that color your observations of the behavior of others. Be aware that those preconceptions have no objective validity; they belong to you.

3. Explore experiences you had earlier in your life that may have led you to forming these preconceptions. Reflect on whether those preconceptions are valid today.

Activities

Drawing on the account you've just read about Natasha's struggle to raise her awareness and let go of long-held stereotypes that have strongly impacted her, think of a time you might have stereotyped another person. Describe in writing the situation or circumstances. Include the stereotypical label you put on the other person in this manner:

- Most (*name the group or category of people*) are (*write the characteristics of that group*).

- Most (*name the group or category of people*) act (*write the behaviors of that group*).

Write what you think caused you to believe that about the person you stereotyped. Here are some possible causes:

- At the time, it seemed to be common knowledge.

- I heard my mother or father say the same thing.

- Someone else whose opinion I respected told me the stereotype was true.

- I heard my friends saying that.

- I formed my opinion on the basis of my own observations at the time.

Since that time, have you come across new information

that contradicts the stereotype with which you labeled the person? If so, summarize the new information. If not, try to find some new information that may contradict the stereotype.

Rethink your stereotype about another person that you described earlier in light of the new information you have received about that stereotype. Write a new statement about that person in the manner that replaces your previous stereotype:

- Some (*name the group or category of people*) may be (*write the characteristics*), but many others in that group may not be.

CHAPTER 3

LISTENING

It is the province of knowledge to speak, and
it is the privilege of wisdom to listen.

—Oliver Wendell Holmes

One of our colleagues was a mental-health professional working with a volunteer organization that helped in disasters. She trained extensively, and yet, after only her third assignment, she decided to throw in the towel because her superiors failed to listen to anything she had to say. "It was a shame that valuable resources were wasted and that I returned early because a few individuals 'in power' lacked the listening skills to effectively address my situation," the colleague, whom we'll call "Cathy," said. Later we will consider how Cathy's superiors might have functioned differently.

Learning how to listen is a skill we are expected to perform at an early age, yet it is a skill that is rarely taught in school. Do you remember being told to "listen" as a small child? As a preadolescent, were you told, "You need to listen!"?

Did your parents yell, *"Listen to me!"* when you were a full-fledged teenager?

If you were a typical teenager, you probably weren't listening when they were yelling. And their yelling didn't encourage you to listen. How could it? You were never given any instructions on listening. Learning to listen simply by observation requires a lifetime of pattern recognition. It is challenging at best. Just as children don't generally learn to read on their own, people don't listen the right way until they've been trained to listen.

Listening, in the simplest sense, involves stepping aside from our own agendas. This is easier said than done. It is not uncommon for us to have feelings come up when someone is speaking to us. These feelings can take our focus away from what the speaker is saying. We're distracted further when we concentrate on how we are going to respond. The needs of the speaker and our own needs can conflict, resulting in very little, if any, listening on our part.

When people use the word "listening," they're referring to the process of hearing words and understanding their literal meaning. But what we do in reality is anything but listen. Much of the time, when one person is talking, the other person is listening only for the purpose of constructing a reply. That "listener" is actively looking for how the words relate to himself and how he can segue into his own stories.

To truly listen to another person, it is key that you give your full attention to that person. At the same time, you must become aware of your thoughts and feelings—and temporarily put them aside. That makes it possible to focus on the speaker. This process can occur repeatedly in a conversation. Noticing when your attention drifts away and then redirecting your focus back to the speaker is a basic ingredient in listening.

As you become more practiced in focusing your attention on the speaker, you lay the foundation for learning additional listening skills. You can become better aware of the need to check in with speakers to make sure you are hearing what they are attempting to communicate. This lets speakers know what you have understood. You might say to a speaker, "This is what came through to me when you were speaking. Is that correct?" By learning how to truly "listen for understanding," you will enter a new world of recognizing how others feel and why they act the way they do.

Listening for Understanding

When you "listen for understanding," it is with a desire to grasp the meaning behind the spoken words. Your aim is to understand the speaker's emotions and the motives behind her statements. This doesn't necessarily mean you intend to agree with the other person or that you want her to change her viewpoint. You are not trying to find solutions. You want to connect with the other person on a level deep enough so you can communicate in a way that leads to better understanding between you.

Simple listening becomes "listening for understanding" when you make an honest and determined effort to hear and digest someone's point of view—and that person's feelings—without making an immediate judgment. It requires an ability to quiet your thoughts and your desire to speak so you really absorb what the other person is saying. Keeping quiet, however, doesn't mean you are not totally participating. Listening for understanding is an active experience.

To be sensitive to other people's emotions, you must pay attention not only to their words but to the tone of their voice, their posture, and their facial expressions. To help you hear and see the nuances of another person's perspective, reflect on what that person might be assuming and how he might be feeling. However, you should not consider your assumptions as true until you verify them with the other person.

Empathy is an essential ingredient in listening for understanding. It draws on the capacity to understand other people's thoughts and to feel their emotions. It is a capacity that is different from sympathy, which involves recognizing other people's circumstances and feeling sorry for them.

When you demonstrate empathy, you are able to stay

present with a person long enough to recognize a possible shift in the initial assumptions you have made about her. You may find that what you thought she was saying at first was completely different from what you eventually learned she was trying to tell you.

Brenda Ueland, a twentieth-century American journalist and radio writer, penned a classic essay, "Tell Me More: On the Fine Art of Listening,"[6] which captures some of the most important elements involved in demonstrating empathy and learning to listen for understanding.

According to Ueland, "Listening, not talking, is the gifted and great role, and the imaginative role." The "true listener," Ueland says, "is much more beloved, magnetic than the talker, and he is more effective and learns more and does more good."

Ueland emphasizes the creative strength inherent in a listener being truly present. It allows people to tell their stories in such a way that they experience being heard, as possibly never before. Listening deeply and giving our undivided attention to other people's accounts helps us connect with emotions behind their words.

We wholeheartedly recommend Ueland's suggestions on truly listening:

---

6   Brenda Ueland, "Tell Me More: On the Fine Art of Listening," in *Strength to Your Sword Arm: Selected Writings* (Duluth, MN: Holy Cow! Press,1992).

Try to learn tranquility, to live in the present part of the time every day. Sometimes say to yourself, "Now. What is happening now? This friend is talking. I am quiet. There is endless time. I hear it, every word."

Then suddenly you begin to hear not only what people are saying but what they are trying to say, and you sense the whole truth about them. And you sense existence not piecemeal, not this object and that, but as a translucent whole.

Ueland advises her readers to listen to their spouses, their parents, their children, and their friends; to "those who love you and those who don't; to those who bore you; to your enemies." It will, she says, "work a small miracle. And perhaps a great one."

A Disaster-Aid Worker Is Rebuffed

There won't be many such miracles when people don't listen to you. Instead, you could easily feel shut off, stymied, and angry. That's how Cathy, our colleague with the disaster-aid group, described the way she felt after her ordeal. Her story is a good lesson on how a failure to listen can affect someone. Here's what happened:

Years ago, I signed up for and received extensive training to volunteer at an emergency response organization. Mental-health professional volunteers are in short supply. Volunteers can expect to get as little as twenty-four hours' notice to work at a disaster and must be willing to be deployed for at least two weeks. This meant that on short notice, I'd have to request several days of vacation from my employer.

On one disaster call, I flew to a state three time zones away, checked in at a hotel, and then reported to the volunteer headquarters. Sam, the assistant mental-health manager and himself a volunteer, greeted me and assigned me to do a three-day "needs assessment" at a center that was a two-hour drive away.

I was concerned about this placement due to safety reasons. I was new to disaster work, having gone on only two previous assignments. Both times I had traveled with other volunteers to the assigned sites. This time I was expected to drive alone to a flooded area.

I told Sam, "I want to do the work, but I'm not sure I can handle it by myself. Can you assign another volunteer to go with me?" He replied, "We're short on volunteers, so

I can't possibly send someone with you. You're a professional. You wouldn't be here if you couldn't do the work. Just get with it and do it."

Still experiencing a queasy feeling in my stomach, I said, "But I've just talked with another assistant mental-health manager who told me she actually did a needs assessment earlier today at the same site. She said mental-health volunteers should not be placed at that site because—"

Sam interrupted me, saying, "That person had no business saying that, and you had no business listening to her. You're working for me, and you need to do what I tell you to do. I'm not going to take any more guff from you. You're going!" Then he abruptly walked away.

I didn't feel Sam made any effort at all to listen to me. He didn't share with me the importance or purpose of the assignment, and he didn't explain why a second needs assessment was necessary.

Here is the Ladder of Assumptions I went up about Sam:

- The **setting** was the volunteer headquarters shortly after a disaster.

- The **facts** were that I was assigned to drive alone to meet with people at the site and to do a three-day needs assessment. An assessment had been done the same day at the same site by an assistant mental-health manager. I spoke to Sam about my concerns about going alone and doing what seemed to be unnecessary work. He said he couldn't change the assignment and that I shouldn't listen to the other volunteer's assessment. His last statement was, "You're going."

- I **interpreted** Sam's response to my attempts to talk to him as rude, unprofessional, and dismissive.

- The **motive** I attributed to Sam was that he felt he knew best, didn't want anyone to question his decisions, and wanted to wield power over me.

- I **stereotyped** him as one of those ill-prepared volunteers who are placed in positions of authority that they never would have held in the professional domain because they lacked the necessary managerial skills.

- My **actions** were to get extremely frustrated and angry. Yet, although ambivalent about the placement, I did what I was told and went alone to the site to do the needs assessment. I did the minimal work required. I saw only eleven clients over the three days I was there.

At the end of the assignment, I was still angry at Sam. I called him to report the minimal activity level and staffing needs at my site. Sam interrupted me and said curtly, "I don't care what you think. There was work there to be done, and there is still more work that needs to be done. I'm the one who makes those decisions, not you. Report to headquarters tomorrow at one p.m." As his tone seemed punitive, I was concerned and asked about my next assignment. He again ordered me to report to headquarters the next day and hung up on me.

Feeling uneasy about the situation, I then called headquarters and asked to speak to Sam's boss, Jill, also a volunteer. I attempted to explain the situation to her, but she interrupted me, saying, "Cathy, you've been a problem from the very beginning. I've received only bad reports about you and your work."

Hurt by her comments, I said, "I've done the best I could under the circumstances. Where did my bad reports come from?" Jill said she received the information from Sam. I felt he'd been rude, unprofessional, and dismissive toward me from the time we met, so it was no surprise that he was the source of the bad reports.

Jill then gave me an ultimatum: "Either stay at your first assignment site and do your job with a smile, or you'll get another bad review and will be sent home." She wanted an answer from me right then. She didn't allow me to explain my experience at my site or give my perspective on the situation.

Because of the level of hostility and lack of respect I felt from both Sam and Jill, I told her, "I'm going home then." She said, "Go ahead, but you'll have to figure out your travel arrangements yourself. I've got my own work to do."

I felt it was a shame that valuable resources

were wasted and that I returned early because a few individuals "in power" lacked the listening skills to effectively address my situation. With that experience behind me, I questioned the effectiveness of the organization in screening volunteers for managerial positions. I sent a letter to the organization, in which I shared my experiences and stated that I was withdrawing as a volunteer for the organization.

Cathy did not feel Sam or Jill listened to her, resulting in the organization's loss of a skilled volunteer. The outcome might have been quite different if Sam and Jill had listened for understanding to Cathy.

Actions That Impede Listening for Understanding

Any number of things can get in the way of listening for understanding when two or more people are supposed to be having a conversation. Here are some actions that can hinder communication:

- when you talk interminably, rarely stopping even to take a breath, giving the other person virtually no space to respond

- when you assume the other person has discounted your views and you respond negatively to what that person is saying

- when you disagree instantly with what a person is saying and justify your opinion as the "correct" one

- when you interrupt a person before she finishes a statement and launch into your own views

- when you immediately follow an individual's account of a personal experience with an experience of your own, without asking the other person if he would be interested in hearing about that experience

- when you tell your side of an issue so strongly that the other person finds you defensive

- when you respond to someone who challenges you by confronting that person in like manner, usually resulting in a "tit for tat" exchange

Over the course of our many mediation sessions, we have developed four techniques that will help you avoid those types of actions and become a good listener. We'll use Cathy's experience to demonstrate the techniques, showing how Sam and Jill might have responded to Cathy as good listeners.

How to Listen for Understanding

1. Encourage

A speaker begins to feel understood when you encourage the person to say more. You do this by asking open-ended questions or by using other ways to request more information. An open-ended question is one that leads to a response greater than a word or two. A closed-ended question can generally be answered with a yes or a no.

When you are asking open-ended questions, you can get a better response from someone if you phrase the question in a manner that allows the respondent to be expressive, encouraging the person to share background information, feelings, and motivations.

Here are examples of open-ended questions:

- What led to the argument you had with him?

- What made you feel that way?

- How did you go about addressing the problem?

- What possibilities for resolving the issues did you consider?

- How did you arrive at the agreement that was reached?

- What factors did you consider when you decided to include that provision in the agreement?

Here are examples of phrases designed to get the speaker to elaborate on what he has just said:

- Tell me more about that.

- I don't fully understand what you've just said.

- I'd like to hear your concerns in somewhat more detail.

- I'd like to know more about how you felt about that.

If Sam and Jill had been listening to Cathy for understanding, this is what they might have said to encourage her to more fully describe her concerns:

> **Sam:** I can tell you're anxious about going on this assignment, Cathy. It's hard for me to fully understand why you're so concerned about going to the site alone. Can you fill me in on what seems to make you so nervous about that? If I can get a better handle on why the assignment is unsettling to you, I might be able to work out a different assignment for you.
>
> **Jill:** I'm glad you called me, Cathy. I need

to have you give me some more details about your experience doing the needs assessment at that site. It will give me more to go on when I decide what we're going to do there next. Also, the way you describe your dealings with Sam concerns me. Please say more about exactly what you said to him and what he said to you. I need to get a better picture of what you said to each other.

When we're willing to step back from a conflict with another person and sincerely invite the person to expand on what has been said, it opens up the possibility of breaking through an impasse and getting to the source of an issue.

2. **Clarify**

To fully grasp the concerns and feelings behind what another person is saying, you have to dig even deeper. Admitting you don't yet have a clear picture of what is bothering the other person is not a bad thing. It actually indicates you are sincerely trying. To listen for understanding, you must then ask clarifying questions to let the other person know you are seriously interested in that person's views.

Here are some examples of questions that are meant to elicit more information:

- What did I do that caused you to feel this way about me?

- I'm not clear about how my behavior affected you. Could you go over your feelings once again?

- You said I couldn't care less about what is going on in your life. Can you explain to me what you meant by that?

Here are some possible clarifying questions Sam and Jill might have asked Cathy, if they had been listening for understanding:

> **Sam:** You said you've had very little experience doing this kind of work in a disaster area, Cathy. Can you tell me what kind of experience you've had doing this kind of work in non-disaster situations? Also, can you describe what type of work you've done in other disaster situations?

> **Jill:** Filling me in on your experience doing the needs assessment at the site and your interactions with Sam has been very helpful, Cathy. What was it the other volunteer told you about her experience earlier in the day at the site that convinced you additional needs assessment work would be redundant? And what was it about Sam's tone of voice and choice of words that caused you to feel he wasn't interested in your side of the story?

3. **Restate**

In a conversation between two people—a dialogue—listening for understanding means both people should feel acknowledged and understood. One of the best ways to make sure you understand another person is by acknowledging the other person. You can do this in two ways:

1. by paraphrasing or restating in condensed form what that person has said and

2. by reflecting a feeling you've picked up from the other person.

These types of statements confirm you are listening to him for understanding:

- It seems what I said made you think I don't respect you.

- It sounds as if you're feeling really frustrated with me right now.

- I gather you feel I've been rude to you.

- From what you've told me, I can tell you're really angry at me.

Here is what Sam and Jill might have restated and reflected to Cathy, if they had been listening to her for understanding:

Sam: You seem worried about going to the site by yourself, Cathy, when you've had very little experience doing this kind of work in a disaster area. You're also wondering whether the work is necessary, given that another volunteer already did a needs assessment there today and told you another one wouldn't be necessary.

Jill: From listening to you, Cathy, I gather you feel you weren't really needed at the site because the activity level was so low, and you were confused about why you were even sent out. I take it your interactions with Sam have been extremely frustrating for you because you felt he treated you in a dismissive manner.

4. Summarize

When you summarize the key perceptions and feelings you think you've heard, it gives the other person a chance to either acknowledge you are right on target, or, if you've missed something, let you know what you didn't catch the first time around. The end result is a level of transparency between you and the other person that puts the other person at ease. Making it clear you have heard someone else's perspective is not the same as agreeing with that person. You may not agree with her view, but you want her to know you have definitely heard it.

Here are several examples of summing-up statements:

- To a student confiding in you about his second thoughts about his college choice: "When the college rep interviewed you during your senior year in high school, you felt good about the college. Now that you've finished your freshman year, you're wondering whether the college really meets your academic needs and whether you should even have accepted its offer of a scholarship."

- To the loved one who has talked to you about what you've done since promising to quit smoking: "You're upset with me because I promised to quit smoking, but I haven't been able to quit completely. You think I never really intended to quit and that I told you I would just to get you off my back."

- To the executive who came to you with his concerns about finances at your firm: "You're angry because Jack, whom you trusted to manage finances, has let you down. To assess the financial status of the company, you've decided you need an impartial financial audit."

Here is how Sam and Jill might have summarized what Cathy said to them, if they had been listening for understanding to her:

Sam: In a nutshell, Cathy, it seems as though

you feel you don't have the experience and skills to carry out the assignment I've given you today. Also, you question whether the three-day needs assessment, which is the central task in the assignment, is necessary because another volunteer has already completed that task. I'd still like you to do another needs assessment to confirm the one that was done today. If we could spare another volunteer, I'd send one with you, but we can't. Do you have any ideas of what else we might do to make you feel safer? I hope I can help you feel comfortable in taking on this assignment.

Jill: I appreciate your being honest about why you didn't want to go to the site on your own and why you were put off by Sam's insistence that you do so. You said the three days you spent at the site could have been spent at a site where you felt you were truly needed. That's the kind of input I need to hear. We need to do a much better job of making good use of the few professional volunteers we have. Do you think it would make sense for the three of us—you, Sam, and me—to talk about this when you get back to headquarters? It'd be good if we could all learn how to do things better based on our recent experiences.

Opening the Door for Discussion

Your intention should always be to listen to someone for understanding, rather than listening only so you can respond. When you listen for understanding, you show the person talking to you that you really care about what she has to say. Your sincere interest has been clear through your words. The other person no longer clings so tightly to her position but starts to open up to you and your perspective.

You have opened the door to a discussion of the factual basis of the assumptions the person has made about you. You have helped the person explore the root causes for her thoughts and to find a path to correcting any erroneous conclusions she may have reached about you. You have, indeed, truly listened for understanding.

Listening intently to another person is hard work. Our colleague Peter Pearson has spent more than twenty years as a therapist helping couples resolve their conflicts. Pearson and his wife, Ellyn Bader, founded the Couples Institute in Menlo Park, California. He's found from his work that "the motivation to listen requires that it be stronger than the self-protect and self-defense mechanism."

There's actually a physiological reason for this, according

to Pearson. He says that when people get defensive, the limbic system in the brain is activated and draws more blood to it. Less blood (oxygen) goes to the analytical, or logical, part of the brain. The logical part of the brain needs to kick in before you can step back and listen for understanding. But when the logical part of the brain gets less oxygen than the limbic system, it interferes with your ability to see things analytically. And you wind up overreacting emotionally.[7]

So what can you do to overcome that emotional reaction? And how can you remember to do it? Pearson recommends you "breathe and breathe again." Pearson says that taking relaxed breaths will send more oxygen to the logical brain. When that happens, you're better able to think. That's the condition you want to be in to take advantage of our suggestions for listening for understanding. Oh, and Pearson has a little tip: stretching your arms will decrease the "fight-or-flight" response.[8]

Sometimes people are reluctant to listen without immediately responding because they don't want to appear to be ceding a point in an argument or giving in. Remember that listening for understanding does not mean you are necessarily agreeing with the other person's point of view or supporting it. Listening for understanding is neither

---

7   Peter Pearson (cofounder, the Couples Institute) in e-mail communication to authors, December 28, 2010.

8   Ibid.

giving advice nor telling people why they shouldn't feel the way they do. It is listening so you understand where the other person is coming from. At this point, you are not trying to solve anything. You are simply paying attention.

When you can communicate to people that you are hearing what they are feeling, no matter how irrational their feelings may seem to be, they can stop trying to justify to you and to themselves what is going on inside them. They can then start down the road of figuring out for themselves the assumptions behind their feelings. Eventually, this process may result in suggestions that benefit both of you. For further examples of the four components of listening for understanding, refer to Appendix I.

Concluding Tips

Listen for understanding by encouraging another person to expand upon what she has been saying to you.

1. Quiet your mind while others are expressing their views about you. Take a deep breath, and let intruding thoughts fade away so you can be in the moment with a speaker.

2. Try to be truly open to others' views about you. Be interested in learning more from others about their views of your strong areas and your areas that need developing.

3. Explore the possibility that others' views are as valid as yours. Keep reminding yourself that your view is one of many regarding a particular situation. Remember that your perspective of any given situation is different from everyone else's.

Listen for understanding by asking clarifying questions of the other person.

1. Be sincerely curious about where others got their information about your behavior. Phrase your question in a manner that indicates you are grateful to receive further information, rather than in a way that might come across as blaming the other person.

2. Be honest in your desire to know how others reached their conclusions about you. Know that others usually aren't purposefully trying to make an incorrect case against you but, rather, have simply raced up their own Ladder of Assumptions about you.

3. Try to help others explore alternative conclusions about your behavior than the ones they drew. Ask them if they might be willing to entertain an explanation for your behavior that they haven't yet considered.

Listen for understanding by restating and reflecting what you have heard from the other person.

1. State in your own words the points you heard from the other person. Work on remembering the essential thoughts expressed by the other person and then putting them into words that come naturally to you.

2. Share with the other person the feelings you heard behind his words. Develop a "third" ear that enables you to get "in tune" with the other person's deeply felt emotions.

3. Keep trying until the person tells you that the points you restated and the feelings you reflected are on target. Don't take personally any statements from another person that might seem to impugn your ability to hear what she is saying. Try, and then try again. You can succeed!

Listen for understanding by summarizing the main points and feelings you heard throughout the other person's account.

1. Pull together and state the key points mentioned by the other person. Practice moving from statements of minute detail you heard from the other person to general statements that capture the essence of what he has said.

2.   Share with the other person the key feelings expressed by the person. From all the various emotions you have heard from the other person, focus strictly on the predominant feelings you have heard, and communicate those.

3.   Continue until the person says you have correctly heard all her key points and feelings. Keep repeating in different ways and rephrasing what you have heard until the other person is satisfied with your grasp of what she has said. Don't stop until the person expresses confidence that you've heard everything she has said.

Activities

Create an image of yourself being a good listener, and give that image a name (a strong word, such as "compassionate").

Write a few guidelines taken from the suggestions in this chapter for listening for understanding.

Step into the shoes of someone with whom you currently are or recently were in a conflict. Complete the following steps, in which you put into practice what you have learned about how to listen for understanding.

Refer to the first two steps in listening for understanding— "encourage" and "clarify"—and then perform these tasks:

- Compose up to three statements or questions aimed at understanding the other person's situation better.

- If possible, arrange some time with the other person.

- Repeat your strong word, and take a deep, relaxing breath.

- Have handy the paper you wrote with the guidelines for listening for understanding.

- Practice making the statements and asking the questions.

Refer to the last two ways to listen for understanding—"restate" and "summarize"—and then perform these tasks:

- Reflect to the other person what you have heard and any feelings you have picked up.

- Summarize what you heard the other person say.

When you first practice these exercises with someone else, they may seem strange and unfamiliar to both of you. So you may want to explain to the other person what you are learning and trying to do. That may help you get that person's buy-in to the process.

CHAPTER 4

CLARIFYING ASSUMPTIONS

Understanding is a two-way street.

—Eleanor Roosevelt

It's hard enough for people who see each other every day to resolve conflicts, but when people are in other parts of the country, unknowns and miscommunication can build up.

Consider the case of a group of coworkers at a company based on the West Coast, whose project was to develop a training class. When one employee, a telecommuter in the Midwest, started missing due dates and failing to reply to e-mails or to return phone calls, one of the other team members got frustrated.

With little information to go on to explain why her coworker had dropped off the map, she assumed the worst: that he was taking advantage of his working from home to blow off the rest of the team.

In this case, our frustrated employee couldn't know what

was going on with her coworker because they weren't communicating and they weren't close enough to each other for one of them to go into the other's office—or even drive to the person's house. We'll delve further into this case later.

In many instances, people who aren't far apart still make unfounded assumptions about each other. In fact, this can happen with coworkers who have offices on the same floor—and even with people living in the same home.

It happens when there isn't full communication between people.

Say you're a freshman in college and you've been having a rough time. You've been stressed about your studies, anxious about your future on the women's varsity soccer team, and spending a lot of time deciding what you need to do to improve your chances of becoming a really good soccer player. You have to deliver news to your roommate that may not be accepted well. Although *you* have known about it for a while, your roommate may feel as though it is coming from left field. You and your roommate are good friends, and you want to keep that friendship. This is, in fact, an amalgam of several cases we mediated.

How might you shape this "must have" discussion to preserve your relationship? Consider if you were to introduce it this way:

You: Erin, Candace and I are going to be roommates next year. I asked her, and she said yes. I wanted to let you know as soon as possible so you could start thinking about what you're going to do for next year.

Erin: Wait. Did I hear you right? Did you say you asked Candace to be your roommate next year?

You: Yeah. Candace agreed to room with me next year. It doesn't have anything to do—

Erin: I didn't have any idea you wanted to change roommates. I thought we were gonna room together again. I thought we were good friends and roomies.

You: We *are* good friends—

Erin: Do you realize this is the end of spring semester? People are studying for finals and packing up to go home for the summer! Finding a new roommate now will be almost impossible, especially since I haven't made any real friends other than you this year. This news is really freaking me out.

You: Erin—

Erin: How am I supposed to ask practical

strangers to be my roommate? I don't know what I'm gonna do if I can't find another roommate.

You completely understand why Erin was so angry with you. You recognize that Erin felt betrayed and tossed aside. Now she's going to work through those feelings and prove to you that you made the wrong decision. But you have read this book, so you are going to try listening for understanding while she makes her case. Here's how that conversation might sound:

> **Erin**: I think you've totally forgotten about all the things I've done for you this year. I never complained when you came in late from a party and turned all the lights on. I took you home with me over spring break so you wouldn't have to stay on campus alone. I've helped you out of all kinds of weird situations. Who else would do all that? Of course I thought we'd be roomies again next year!

> **You**: You think I haven't noticed or appreciated all you've done for me this year.

> **Erin**: Not only that, but you've gone behind my back to find another roommate! At least you could have given me the courtesy of telling me what you were up to. I had no idea

how devious and underhanded you are. You sure had me fooled. I thought we had a good relationship, but apparently we don't.

You: So you're mad at me for finding a different roommate for next year without telling you what I was planning. And you think I've been sneaky.

Erin: I feel so betrayed. Who can you trust these days?

You: I'm guessing my actions have made you feel let down and dumped. Is that what you're feeling?

Erin: Yeah, that's *exactly* the way I feel.

By listening carefully to Erin, you have a good grasp on why she interpreted your statement about rooming with Candace next year as a rejection of her. Erin's interpretation of your statement leaves you feeling a bit guilty because it truly was not your intention to diminish her in any way. You also are feeling that this conversation seems incomplete. Something is missing.

You may feel frustrated because you have not had an opportunity to tell your side of the issue. Erin has not given you the opportunity to really explain your rationale, which is clearly different from what she is thinking. You listened to Erin, but she has not returned the favor by listening to you. Maybe Erin doesn't know that listening is a two-way street. It is now your job to help her listen to you.

Both parties in a conflict need to listen to each other for understanding. Without each party being heard, reaching a final agreement that resolves their conflict may be next to impossible.

Completing the Listening Cycle

How can you motivate Erin to listen to your side of the story? And why is it so important for you to be heard? Why can't you just be satisfied with having heard her side of the story?

Erin felt the weight of anger driven by miscommunication lifted off her when she felt you listened to her. It is also important for *you* to lighten *your* emotional load by explaining the rationale for your comment that unintentionally came across to her as being hurtful.

The hurdle you are facing now is figuring out how to encourage Erin to listen to your perspective. Fortunately, there are two beneficial circumstances in your favor that you have already set up by having listened to Erin first:

1. Erin feels you listened to her, though she probably still feels somewhat resentful of you. She may not feel compelled to remain in what is essentially a

fight-or-flight scenario. Now her mind, heart, tone of voice, and body language may be more open.

2.   You have just modeled how to listen for understanding by listening intently to Erin. She may find it easier to listen for understanding to you by mirroring your listening lead.

Making the Approach to Being Heard

Once you have listened thoughtfully to Erin, you might take the following approach:

Let Erin know you would like to have another discussion with her about the situation. Asking takes courage. You want to clear the air. You don't want Erin to stay hurt and mad at you. So you want her to hear you out about your reasons for getting a new roommate. To Erin, those reasons may turn out to be questionable. But remember, you are asking Erin to join you in your pursuit of a resolution to the situation. In response to your showing respect for her, your hope is that she will agree to work with you in seeking to resolve the issues dividing the two of you.

You might start by telling Erin that you didn't mean to shock her. Ask her if you can share your thinking about changing roommates. In effect, you are asking Erin to help you explore the factual basis of your assumptions. Describe to her your reasons and values, and ask her to recap them without judgment, as you did for her in the first discussion.

You: Erin, the more I think about what you said, the more I get where you're coming from. At first I was surprised by how you reacted, but now I totally get why you're mad at me. I realize the way I brought this up was really insensitive. Are you up for listening to what I meant to say?

Erin: I heard what you said the first time. You want to room with Candace. Period. You seem to have forgotten all the things I did to help you with school and your personal life.

You: I can totally see how you feel that way. Will you give me a chance to explain?

Erin (reluctantly): Okay.

You: The reason I asked Candace to be my roommate definitely has nothing to do with you. You've helped me a lot with my classes and when I was struggling with being away from home for the first time. I asked Candace because we have the same classes and the same major. We also have the same tough workout schedule. You know how Candace and I are on the soccer team. If we live together, I'm sure she'll give me tips about how I can get my game on. And maybe I can help her. You know how this season was a bummer 'cause I didn't get to actually play much, and I'd really like to be a starter next year. I was thinking Candace would help me.

At this point, you want to check in with Erin to find out what she heard you say and how she feels about your explanation.

You: Does that make sense?

Erin: Well, I'm no soccer player, so I can see how living with Candace might help you get better. That's your choice, and I guess you didn't mean to put me down. But ... whatever. You were way late in letting me know.

Communicating Constructively

Communicating constructively to another person about your concerns, as you did with Erin, makes it possible to express yourself in a positive, factual way. Otherwise, the way you express yourself could easily put others on the defensive. When you react brusquely to another person's words or behavior and instantly state your opinions, you risk cutting that person off. This does not allow the other person to open up and hear your thoughts, which is what is needed if conflicts are to be transformed into compassionate dialogues where both people feel understood.

To keep the line of communication open, you need to catch yourself before you launch into saying something the other person may consider a verbal attack or that you may later regret. When you notice you are getting angry or agitated, it's a clue your response is not likely to have a positive effect on the other person. You will be more productive if you back off from what the other person may consider harsh or opinionated language.

You may need to postpone talking with the other person until you have been able to reflect on the impact your words and tone may have. Given the outcome you're looking for, what will be the best approach to take? How would you like *her* to talk with *you* if the roles were reversed? Is she likely to react to your words the same way you would react to them, coming from her? Or is she likely to be more receptive to an approach that is different from one that would work for you? We're separate individuals, so we respond differently to the same events and words.

When it's time to give your side, speak openly and directly. Your goal is not to persuade but to have your concerns heard fairly. You want to help the other person understand your assumptions. Your goal is to help her understand how you came to think what you were thinking.

It's not easy to share negative conclusions and judgments you've made. You know they may put off the other person. The key to communicating constructively is to start by sharing what you see as facts and by stating your assumptions clearly and without blame. Once you've shared your point of view, you can ask the other person to share his or her views regarding the accuracy of what he or she just heard.

Clarifying Assumptions

When you and Erin have shared your respective assumptions with each other, you are ready to have a conversation about which assumptions are correct and which are not. Here's how that might go:

> **You**: Erin, your assumption that I'm clueless about all you've done for me isn't true. You've been the best roommate. You've helped me get through some really difficult times this year.

> **Erin**: Thanks. It's kind of hard to believe you, though. I feel—felt, whatever—totally rejected, and it's hard to let go of that feeling. It's cool that you're saying that's not what you meant, that you weren't rejecting me.

> **You**: What do you think, though, about why I want to room with Candace? Do you think it'll help me get better at soccer? I really think so, but maybe I'm wrong.

> **Erin**: Actually, I don't think it really matters.

It's not like you're playing soccer in your dorm room. Personally, I think you just need more confidence and to figure things out for yourself. You're actually a brilliant soccer player.

You: Thanks. That's nice of you to say. I don't think I'm so brilliant at soccer. Hmmm. Maybe I could've gotten better without living with Candace. Who knows what she's like to actually live with? You've got a point that I need to rely on myself more.

Erin: Now that you explained things, I guess maybe you weren't being devious and sneaky.

You: I wasn't trying to be sneaky at all. Candace and I had become such good teammates that I was just thinking about how we could spend more time together next year. It never was about keeping you in the dark. It never occurred to me you might feel like I went behind your back.

Erin: Even though I know you're on the soccer team, I never realized how important it was in your life. It seems soccer's the most important thing to you. Is that it?

You: Hmm. Most important? I don't know. I definitely see myself as a soccer player, and I want to be an absolutely great soccer player. I'm really hoping to play professionally after I graduate.

Erin: Well, it sounds like you think rooming with Candace is going to somehow help you get toward your goal of playing professionally. I just hope we can stay friends, even though we won't be roommates anymore.

You: I sure hope so. I realize now that I told you about my plans way late. I can see how it's gonna make it hard for you to find another roommate. Actually, I can help you look for a roommate. I know a couple of freshmen who are looking for new roommates, and I think you'd be really compatible. And you're right. I could have probably figured out on my own how to be a better soccer player. I might not have had to change roommates to figure that out.

Clarifying Assumptions Is a Process

It isn't always possible to clear the air in one conversation. It can be a step-by-step process in which a series of constructive exchanges occur. It helps to acknowledge that your assumptions are guesses that can turn out to be partly true or not true at all. The point of stating your assumptions to another person is to find out if those assumptions make sense to that person. Eventually, when both of you are willing to give up your unfounded assumptions and focus strictly on the ones that are grounded in reality, you are poised to clear up the misunderstandings between you and move forward toward resolution.

It usually takes time to sort out the assumptions that both of you can agree are unfounded and those that have a basis in fact. In this process of sharing your own assumptions with each other, each of you may also make some discoveries about your own thinking processes.

Conflict on a Geographically Dispersed Team

When the long-distance telecommuter we referred to at the beginning of the chapter went incommunicado, our frustrated employee, whom we'll call Pat, made a number of assumptions in a vacuum. Those assumptions didn't help resolve the conflict. Pat and two other people were at her company's West Coast headquarters; another employee was in an East Coast field office; and "James" worked out of his home in Omaha, Nebraska.

Here's how Pat describes the circumstances:

> We had weekly team teleconference calls
> to discuss the status of our project and the
> development of the training class, and we

had come up with action items. A lot of the work was exchanged via e-mail and attached documents. Input was coming in on the project almost daily. James participated in the calls and had just as many good ideas as any other team member. He also had specialized experience in one subject of the class. No one else had that knowledge.

Then, for days on end, James didn't e-mail anything or return calls. There were action items he had with due dates he missed and didn't explain why. The rest of us, and our two managers, were frustrated, especially because there wasn't much other than e-mailing or calling that we could do with a remote teammate. We couldn't go into his office and talk with him. Sometimes James didn't seem to have done any work between meetings.

As we got closer to an upcoming deadline, before our nine a.m. team conference call, we received a burst of work in an e-mail from James, which came with an eight thirty timestamp. He was in a time zone two hours ahead of us, so that was ten thirty his time. No one had time to read or review his contributions, and consequently, we couldn't discuss them at the meeting. I sarcastically pointed that out, saying, "Thanks for finally sending your work—not that we had any chance of actually reviewing it." I made a few other snide, short comments to James during the meeting. I'm not a screamer; I'm more of a sit-and-fume type, and sarcastic comments help release my irritation.

When I considered the situation later, this is what I realized was my Ladder of Assumptions about James:

- The **setting** was that James and I were coworkers on a five-person team working on developing a training class. We worked via e-mails and phone calls and met as part of a team in a weekly teleconference call.

- The **facts** were that James did not e-mail or call over a period of three weeks. He did call in for the teleconference calls. He e-mailed a large amount of work shortly before deadline and our team call. We didn't have time to review it.

- I **interpreted** James's behavior as inconsiderate, irresponsible, and unprofessional.

- The **motive** I attributed to him was that James worked from home because he wanted it all—a high-paying job in a state with a low cost of living, near his in-laws, who could babysit. But he didn't want to work. He didn't care about letting down the team. He wanted to hide from the consequences of his behavior when he didn't do what he said he'd do.

- I **stereotyped** him as one of those employees who work from home; who have young children not yet in school; and who just don't dedicate their time and focus the way those of us who go into our offices to work do.

- My **actions** were that I was snippy with James at the teleconference. I gossiped about him at work with the other two local coworkers on the team, and I complained to James's boss about his behavior.

After a few days passed and my irritation finally subsided, I felt I could and should deal with this issue by talking with James about my concerns. Because I had taken the action of talking to James's boss, I felt she might have communicated with him, and I was more optimistic that he would either directly answer or return a phone call from me.

James and I did manage to connect on the phone. I felt as if it were one small step in the right direction. He was making himself available. We chatted and made small talk at first. I learned he was remodeling his house and his mother-in-law had recently been very ill for a short while. I used that as an opening to encourage him to communicate with the rest of us. We didn't need to know the personal details about his circumstances, but it helped to know there was something unusual going on.

We went on to talk about the frustration those of us at headquarters felt when he didn't follow through on his actions and he simultaneously went incommunicado. I praised him for his knowledge of the subject matter and the quality of work he did when he turned work in. After actually talking to and hearing from him, I realized he did care about this project and about pulling his weight on the team. When I hadn't been able to communicate at all with him, it was easy for me to assume he didn't care.

I requested he agree only to action items and deadlines he felt he could reasonably make and discuss it with us if he didn't think his assignments made sense. And I asked him, if he couldn't make a deadline, to please let us know ahead of that deadline. The main thing I asked for was for him to communicate, at the least to return calls from us, within a work day.

Pat realized that although her phone call with James wasn't a part of a planned strategy, she had definitely gone through the mental steps of going back down to the factual rung of her Ladder and clarifying her assumptions. She didn't share and check out with James every one of the assumptions she had made earlier. But in the course of their discussion, her opinions changed, and she was able to work out ideas with him to go forward.

Concluding Tips

Ask the person with whom you're in conflict to share his assumptions about you.

1. Move away from your strong feelings and realize your adversaries are human beings. Acknowledge the other person is someone whose story is as legitimate as your own.

2. Try to be truly open and listen with understanding to the other person's views about your behavior.

3. Make your best effort to avoid immediately judging as wrong what you hear from the other person.

Share with the other person the assumptions you've made about him.

1. Try to avoid accusations when you speak to the other person. Be aware that your assumptions may be faulty and are only guesses.

2. Endeavor to state your assumptions without trying to justify them.

3. Take responsibility for the assumptions you've made about the other person and for the effects your assumptions may have had on him.

Ask questions that will help you and the other person determine the factual basis of the assumptions you have made about each other.

1. Be open to receiving new information from the other person about your assumptions without immediately judging that information as wrong.

2. Work toward being able to entertain two contradictory assumptions at the same time—yours and those of the other person.

3. Maintain an attitude of respect toward the other person as you ask questions. Be aware that others can be just as sure they are right about their assumptions as you have been about yours.

Come to agreement with the other person on assumptions that are factually based.

1. Seek to avoid holding on to unnecessary disagreements. Recognize that sticking to assumptions you are convinced are right, without honestly taking into consideration the other person's assumptions, is a stumbling block to reaching an agreement.

2. Shift from thinking, *I'm right and you're wrong* to thinking, *Together we can agree on what is true about our relationship.* Be willing to reshape your assumptions or even abandon them completely if they don't add up

3. Affirm the principle that resolving conflicts and restoring relationships are higher values than being right.

Give your best effort to letting go of invalid assumptions and reaching common ground.

1. Assess whether you sincerely desire to reach common ground with the other person. Search

within yourself to locate any vestiges of angry feelings toward the person.

2. Acknowledge you have sufficient self-confidence to yield to the correctness of another person's assumptions without feeling personally diminished.

3. View the other person as willing to entertain that his assumptions may not necessarily be correct. Consider the other person may be just as flexible as you are.

4. Work hard together at reconciling apparently contradictory assumptions. Search for and find common themes that have been hidden in seemingly opposing assumptions.

Activities

1. Create Erin's Ladder of Assumptions about "you."

2. Create the Ladder of Assumptions "you" made about Erin.

3. This chapter's last scenario, the conflict in a geographically dispersed team, is told from Pat's perspective. Put yourself in James's shoes. What do you think might have been going on with him? Try these scenarios:

- What might have been James's Ladder of Assumptions? What assumptions might he have had about Pat?

- What language could he use to constructively communicate his perspective to Pat? How might he possibly share and check out any assumptions he has?

- Create a realistic script in which they clarify their perspectives and check out assumptions. Continue the dialogue between James and Pat to the point where both are satisfied they've explored the validity of their respective assumptions.

CHAPTER 5

APOLOGIZING AND REACHING AGREEMENT

Apologizing is one of the most powerful tools we have available to deal with conflict in our lives.

—Michelle Gousie Geremia

Rob and Ann sat across from each other discussing problems they were having regarding dinnertime. Rob cooked dinner for the two during the week and was ready to eat when the food was cooked, but Ann's schedule depended on her workload. They wanted to eat together, but Rob couldn't count on Ann being home at a certain time. And Ann faced an irritated partner if she stayed too long finishing her work for the day. Things were stewing for a while before they finally came to a head, about which you will read more later.

We can often help people reach thoughtful solutions that meet both sides' needs. That's what we do. But sometimes it's difficult to identify just what those needs are. Whose needs hadn't been met? Who was at fault? Who should apologize to whom?

Crafting an Effective Apology

Often you know in your gut when you've made an assumption that is wrong about another person. A feeling of dread can come over you, and you know you owe the other person an apology. As mediators, we see the power of sincerely made apologies. You might still face a long struggle before you finally come to terms with each other, but an apology can ease tension and help make people willing to work together. It's as if an invisible blockage has just dissolved, and the ensuing terms of agreement are easier to forge.

It's the same way when a conflict involves someone close to you. Simply saying, "I'm sorry," is not going to cut it. An insincere apology can make you come off as condescending and hinder any progress in resolving your troubles. Without the skill to properly express to the other person that you're sorry, you can turn something that began as a minor offense into a major blow to your relationship.

Fortunately, you can learn how to apologize in a way that is meaningful and constructive.

Sharing the Evening Meal

Before Rob and Ann could sort out their troubles and apologize, they had to understand the seeds of their conflict. Their evening routine had evolved without their formalizing what they did. It had been fine when Ann was to come home around 7:00 p.m. However, it was when her schedule became increasingly irregular and she began coming home later that the two had had tense evenings.

The couple filled in the details. Rob got home by 5:30 p.m., while Ann tended to come home any time between 6:30 and 8:30, depending on her workload. When she came home, Ann would often want to open the mail, check a few things on the computer, and just unwind a little before eating. Rob preferred to eat at 6:30 because he was hungry. The hungrier he was, the more annoyed he got. Rob told us he didn't want to impose a time when Ann came home, but without a set time, he never knew when he should have dinner ready.

When Ann would come home around 8:30, she would find a grouchy partner. By that time, dinner had been simmering for at least an hour. Ann could tell right away from Rob's body language that he was irritable. He banged around the kitchen more than he had to and promptly put the dishes on the table and started eating without talking to or looking at her.

Ann didn't physically get hungry or irritated the way Rob

did, so she couldn't quite empathize with him. Rob felt as if he never knew what to expect. When Ann's late nights became more frequent, Rob felt disrespected and taken for granted. Ann felt pressured to come home and knew that when she did get home, Rob would nag her. It irritated her because she had work pressures, and instead of having a partner who supported her dealing with those pressures, she had one who piled on additional stress and friction at home.

Here is an example of Rob's Ladder of Assumptions about Ann on an evening when there was a blowup:

- The **setting** was Rob and Ann's home in the evening after both had returned from work.

- The **facts** were that Rob had finished making dinner at 7:00 and had it simmering until Ann came home at 8:30. In the previous four workdays, Ann had come home at 6:50, 7:24, 7:10 and 8:05.

- Rob **interpreted** Ann's behavior as inconsiderate, disrespectful and uncaring.

- The **motive** Rob attributed to Ann was that she valued her work more than she valued him and that she took him for granted.

- In this situation, Rob didn't reach the **stereotype** or generalization rung of his Ladder.

- Rob's **actions** were to bang around the kitchen and to avoid eye contact and conversation with Ann during dinner.

Who Should Apologize?

Imagine you're the one mediating the dispute. How do you think Ann should respond to Rob's sulky behavior? She may feel responsible for the situation at home and want to apologize, but she's also feeling justified because she has legitimate reasons for coming home at different times. She thinks Rob could certainly have been more understanding and flexible, and there was no reason he had to be such a grouch and nag her.

How should Rob respond? You know he doesn't mean to create so much drama for Ann when she comes home late, but he feels neglected. Rob feels Ann considers her work more important than their relationship. He feels responsible for the bad vibe, but he also thinks Ann should try harder to place his needs and wants above her work.

Apologies from both Rob and Ann, provided they are effective apologies, could help ease the tension and put them on the path to common ground. Aaron Lazare, MD, a psychiatrist and former dean of the University of Massachusetts Medical School has written *On Apology*,[9] an entire book about apologies, analyzing the factors that

---

9   Aaron Lazare, *On Apology,* (New York City: Oxford University Press, 2004).

lead people to apologize and exploring how people transfer power in apologies. Lazare found that to be effective, most apologies need to contain the following elements:[10]

- acknowledgment of the offensive behavior
- an explanation
- genuine expression of remorse
- making amends

Those factors can help you craft an apology that will go a long way toward bringing people together. If you were Ann, how might you apologize to Rob? Here are examples of effective and ineffective apologies that Ann might have made, based on Lazare's four essential elements.

Acknowledging the Offensive Behavior

To acknowledge your offensive behavior effectively, you must start by describing exactly what you did wrong, including even the worst aspects. Use accurate language. Accept responsibility. This is an essential first step in putting things right.

---

10 Aaron Lazare, "Making Peace Through Apology, "*Greater Good: Magazine of the Center for the Development of Peace and Well-Being*, Volume I, Issue 2, Fall 2004, 16–19.

Ineffective acknowledgment	Effective acknowledgment
"I know I was kind of late tonight. It won't happen again."	"I appreciate that you make dinner for us every night. It must be hard to time dinner when you never know when I'm coming home. I'm sorry I came home so late. I should have been more considerate and called you earlier, so you could decide what you wanted to do about dinner."

Explaining Your Actions

Once you've admitted you did something wrong, the person you've hurt will probably want to know why you acted the way you did. Being truthful is the best way to rebuild a strong, viable relationship. Look within and be honest with yourself. That's key to figuring out the real explanation for your actions, and it will help you change for the better.

Explanations also help reassure both of you that the offense isn't likely to happen again. Excuses, on the other hand, merely signal that you're avoiding responsibility. Leave them out of your apology.

Ineffective explanation	Effective explanation
"Work's such a pain. There's always some fire drill."	"You know that important project with the Friday deadline I told you about? The shipment came in today with only half the parts. My boss called an impromptu meeting right before I was going to leave at 6:30. Then I had some immediate action items I had to take care of after the meeting. I honestly lost track of what time it was. When I saw it was after 8:00, I rushed home, feeling bad that I was going to be late."

Expressing Remorse

It is important that you express real remorse. You've probably heard the "I'm saying this because I should, not because I believe it" apology many times. It doesn't make you feel good because it removes the blame from the person apologizing and puts it on you. If you think the person who offended you isn't remorseful, you're not going to buy the apology. You're only going to feel more offended than ever.

Ineffective expression of remorse	Effective expression of remorse
"I'm sorry it's so late, but I couldn't help it. You're hungry and that's why you're grouchy."	"I'm really sorry I came home so late when you had dinner waiting. As soon as I saw you, I could tell you had been waiting for me. It's so nice to come home to a home-cooked meal. I know you're hungry much earlier, and I appreciate that you always wait for me, so we can eat together. I don't mean to act as if I take you for granted. I'm truly sorry."

Making Amends

Often there will be nothing overt to mend. Hearts and relationships are broken more often than physical objects. Making amends has tremendous healing power, sometimes mending even seemingly irreparable wounds. Merely saying you're sorry is as ineffective as glue. Your actions have to show the person how you feel. A good way of doing this is simply doing what the other person has asked you to do. When you do that, you're showing the other person you have heard him and value him.

Ineffective amends	Effective amends
"I'll try to come home earlier."	"I'll try to be home by 7:30. You can just plan on serving dinner at 7:30. We'll just both count on dinner at 7:30, even if I come home earlier. I know you're hungry earlier, so maybe you can have a snack to help you hold out until 7:30. If I'm not home by then, just eat without me. I'll call when I leave work so you'll know when to expect me. If I know it'll be after 7:30, I'll call you before 7:30 and let you know."

It might help to do a reality check. Both of you will have to figure out whether what the person making amends is offering is realistic and doable, or whether she needs to consider another alternative. That's because if it turns out she can't follow through, her broken promises can make things worse.

If you make an apology that demonstrates honesty about your shortcomings and commitment to doing better, the other person may realize your behavior was unintentional and not intended to cause a conflict. It opens a door for the other person to stop taking your behavior personally.

Was That Apology Real?

Suppose you're on the receiving end of the apology, and the words the other person says feel weak. You may feel worse than before. And you may find yourself being irritated with the other person. The guidelines in this chapter can help you recognize why the apology felt so unsatisfactory. After you read the guidelines, you can then follow up with the person in a positive way. You can use the tips we offer in chapter 4, "Clarifying Assumptions," to learn how to communicate constructively.

When you receive an apology that is sincere and helpful in restoring your relationship, you know it. You get a sixth sense about it. It makes you feel good. It can soothe the hurt you've been feeling and can stop—or even reverse—the damage. It opens the door for you to be able to accept the apology.

Apologies can certainly help pave the way for reaching some sort of agreement. You may discover, however, that you don't need to receive an apology to come to peace about the situation. Through introspection and using the Ladder of Assumptions, you can stop taking the other person's behavior personally. You can release the grievances, wounds, hurts, or feelings of being wronged, recognizing that the behavior was not intentionally hurtful.

Moving toward Agreement

Timing matters when you're trying to reach agreement. Regardless of whether an apology has been made—or made and not accepted—there will come a time when you want to look ahead at what you'd like to see take place.

It helps to wait until both sides have calmed down. When Rob and Ann reach a point at which they are willing to solve the problem instead of bickering, they increase their chances of being able to discuss the situation, listen to each other's ideas about possible solutions, and come up with a solution that works for both of them.

You hear the expression "win-win" a lot—for good reason. It refers to thoughtful solutions that meet the needs of both sides in a dispute. It's not always easy to identify those needs. It's important to keep talking with each other to recognize each other's "needs" and "wants." The two aren't the same.

Needs are essentials, things you cannot do without. Good examples are food, water, and clothing, which people need to maintain a healthy life. *Wants* are things we desire or would like to have but aren't absolutely necessary. Getting take-out pizza and beer is, generally speaking, a "want." A winter jacket for the snow is most likely a "need." A new jacket to change your wardrobe or complement the color of your other clothes and accessories is probably a "want."

When two sides are in a dispute, a good resolution is one that meets the needs of both of you. To discover what those are, it's helpful to brainstorm together. In brainstorming, you put all ideas on the table—even "crazy" ones or ones that need to be fleshed out—without judgment. Both people agree not to judge or criticize the other's suggestions. A kernel of a solution that satisfies both of you may be somewhere underneath all your ideas.

Building Durable Agreements

Peter Pearson, the cofounder of the Couples Institute, says the two most common negotiating mistakes people in conflict make are these:

1. stubbornly pushing for their own interest and

2. submitting too quickly to the other person's suggestions for the sake of avoiding tension.

"The best way to avoid either of these negotiating errors," he says, "is by making suggestions that incorporate benefits for both yourself and the other person."[11]

Negotiating the wrong way could have left Ann and Rob with a simple but unsatisfying solution, such as, "You eat after you get home, and I'll eat after I get home." But

---

11 Peter Pearson (cofounder, the Couples Institute), in e-mail communication to authors, September 11, 2010.

participating in a creative brainstorming conversation can be far more satisfying and long lasting.

Here's how that conversation might go:

> **Ann**: I'll try to be home by 7:30. You can just plan on serving dinner at 7:30, even if I come home earlier. Will that work for you?

> **Rob**: I guess ... but you said you like to have some time to unwind a bit before sitting down to dinner. I realize you need to have that time, but I'm usually very hungry and don't think I can wait for you to unwind.

> **Ann**: Well, if I get home earlier than 7:30, I'll probably have enough time to relax before we eat at 7:30. If I don't get home until 7:30 or after that, I'm fine with your going ahead and eating before I do.

> **Rob**: But I'd like us to set aside the time to eat dinner together, no matter when you get home. We usually have our best talks at the dinner table.

> **Ann**: That's sweet of you to say. Yeah, you're right. How about this? If I get home at 7:30 or later, go ahead and eat. But maybe you could wait to eat your dessert until I get home and have a chance to catch my breath. When I

eat dinner, you can have your dessert, and we can talk about our day.

Rob: That might work. Right after dinner I'm usually too full to really enjoy my dessert anyway. That's probably the best solution for those days you come home after 7:30.

Ann: As I said, though, I'm hoping to be home for 7:30 dinner, with time enough to relax beforehand. And maybe both of us could hold off on dessert for a while. Like you, I think I enjoy it more when I have a little break after dinner.

Rob: Let's give it a try and see how it goes. I'll write down what we've agreed to do so we can look at it later if we need to.

Try your agreement as an experiment rather than as a permanent solution, as Ann and Rob agreed to do in the script above. These interchanges might seem stilted and awkward at first, but you are learning important listening and negotiating skills that will open the way for you to solve this problem and others in your future. When you work together like this toward a mutually agreeable solution, it creates a good feeling of joint ownership and commitment to the resolution you've created.

It can be helpful to put agreements into writing so everyone is clear. In the course of the discussions you have with each other, jot down the points you agree on as you go along. At the end of your conversation, review these points and see whether you still agree with them. Some may need to be changed or deleted, and more items may be needed in your list to fully spell out your decisions.

Try for balance in your agreement so neither of you feels you're giving more than the other. Both need to feel comfortable with what you've agreed to do.

Check whether each item is really doable. Is there anything that would get in the way of carrying out any of the points in your plan? For example, what if one of you will be traveling during the time you agreed to do something? You may not be able to comply with that part of your agreement, so you'll need to agree on a different date.

In writing your agreement, use simple, clear language that both of you understand. If either isn't sure about something, say it in a different way that both of you can understand and agree on. The point is to make sure both know what each expects of the other.

Also consider what will happen if someone doesn't or can't fulfill a portion of the agreement. And put it in writing. Include a contingency, such as contacting the other person when you can't do what you promised to do.

Concluding Tips

Apologize sincerely for making unfounded assumptions about another person.

1. When you have offended another person, acknowledge what you did. Take responsibility for the effects your attitudes, beliefs, and actions had on the other person.

2. Say why you acted the way you did. Be truthful.

3. Express regrets for what you did that was hurtful to the other person. Be truly apologetic.

4. Make a sincere effort to right any wrongs you have committed. Do whatever you can to help the other person recover emotionally from what you did.

Reach agreement with an offended person about ways the two of you can communicate more compassionately in the future.

1. Suggest solutions that will benefit you and the other person. Try to look at the other person's gain as your own gain and his loss as your own loss.

2. From the very start, believe your suggestions for improving the relationship are as worthy as hers. Understand that yielding too quickly to another person's suggestions is counterproductive.

3. Avoid digging in your heels and imposing your ideas on the other person. Be part of the solution rather than part of the problem.

Activities

*   Create an apology Rob could make to Ann that includes the four effective elements of an apology described earlier in this chapter.

*   For examples of individuals who demonstrated giving effective apologies in conflict situations in which they were involved, read Appendices II and III.

CHAPTER 6

GOING IT ALONE

I am only one, but I am one. I cannot do everything, but I can do something; I will not refuse to do the something that I can do.

—Edward Everett Hale

One situation involved a woman who had looked forward to her adult daughter's coming to stay with her at Christmastime. The visit didn't turn out the way the mother had hoped. Her daughter didn't want to participate in the activities her mother had planned and abruptly ended her stay. The daughter was gone, but the conflict remained. The mother wanted to resolve the dispute, but here she had to go it alone. You will read later in the chapter how she resolved it.

What happens when there is no way for you to talk it out with someone?

There are times when one person in a conflict wants to reach resolution but the other party is unavailable or unwilling to share and clarify assumptions. There are even times when the person who committed the perceived offense dies before the other person has come to terms with obstacles in the relationship.

There are things you can do yourself. You can figure out on your own how not to take the other person's reactions personally. You can learn how to defuse your hurt and angry feelings resulting from the negative assumptions you make about the other person's behavior

A Conflict with a Dinner Partner

Maureen contacted us because she needed assistance in resolving a very negative confrontation she'd had with another person in her retirement community. It wasn't the type of situation where she wanted to talk directly with the person. And she didn't need to. Working with us, Maureen was able to clarify her assumptions about the man—and overcome her hurt and angry feelings—without ever engaging in a dialogue with him.

Here's what happened, in Maureen's words:

> I live at a retirement community. Early on, I was invited to join several single men and women for dinner. They typically eat together in the common dining room. Occasionally, a member of the group makes plans to eat dinner with someone else. And sometimes we invite another single person to eat with

us. We usually gather at a table for about forty-five minutes for a glass of wine before sitting down to dinner in the dining room.

One evening, we were seated at a table enjoying our wine and talking with each other. At one point, I walked into the dining room to speak to the maître d' about reserving a dinner table. As I was doing so, a single man, who occasionally eats with us, also walked up to the maître d'. I invited Sam to join us for dinner, and he accepted.

I walked back to where we were seated and brought a chair up to the table to my right for Sam. As Sam sat down, Brian, who was sitting in the chair to the right of Sam, stood up and shouted past Sam directly at me, saying, "F— off!"

I was shocked to my core. No one had ever said that to me before. My father never permitted vulgar language like that to be spoken in our home. I couldn't imagine what would have caused Brian to speak to me in such a demeaning way. I could see the others at the table staring at Brian, and I was sure they had heard what he had shouted at me.

Shortly, everyone got up and walked into the dining room. I was the last one to walk to the dinner table. By that time, there was only one vacant chair, which happened to be to Brian's right. I sat in it. I was still in a total state of disbelief about what Brian had said to me.

Brian leaned toward me and said so softly that no one else could hear him, "I'm sorry." I'd heard what he said, but I didn't acknowledge I had heard him. To me, it seemed a perfunctory statement with no feeling behind it. It seemed as though he was simply trying to be dutiful.

Throughout dinner I said nothing, though I'm usually quite talkative. I left the table before dessert was served and went to my apartment, still speechless and in a state of utter shock. I spent a sleepless night, trying to figure out what I had said or done that could possibly have caused Brian to explode at me the way he had.

My conflict with Brian totally devastated me for a week after that. Day after day and night after night, I struggled with my feelings of having been deeply offended by Brian's remark and of being very angry at him.

Finally, I was able to sit at my desk and write on a pad of paper the assumptions about Brian that had initially crossed my mind.

Here is a description of my Ladder of Assumptions:

- The **setting** was the dining room of our retirement facility.

- The **facts** were that a group of men and women were sitting at a table. Later, we were joined by another man. At that point, a man who was already seated at the table spoke to me. Later, the group of us ate dinner together at a table in the dining room. I said nothing to the man who had spoken to me, and I left the table before dessert was served.

- I **interpreted** the comment of the man who spoke to me earlier as harsh, vulgar, unwarranted, and deeply offensive.

- The **motive** I attributed to him was that he resented me for rejecting him as a friend because I had invited another man to join us for dinner.

- I **stereotyped** him as one of those men who are socially inept and who are

121

possessive about women for whom they have positive feelings.

- My **actions** were that I virtually went incommunicado and walked away from the situation as soon as I comfortably could. For the following week, I tried to dig myself out of my pit of depression that followed the incident.

After several days had passed, I was able to refer to my Ladder of Assumptions about Brian to help calm myself down. I could see what the facts were and what my assumptions were. Even though I never checked my assumptions with Brian, examining my Ladder helped me see that what he had said may have had more to do with him than with anything I had said or done.

Eventually, my hurt feelings faded away, and I no longer felt angry toward him. However, for the time being, I thought it best if I didn't eat with my dinner group when Brian was at that table.

Never having dealt with a situation like this before, I found it hard to imagine feeling comfortable sitting with Brian at that dinner table again. In time, however, I came to the realization that I might be able to do so if I moved out and broadened my circle of friends. This would enable me to eat with a number of different groups at different times.

Feeling I no longer would be obligated to eat every night with that same group eased a lot of the tension that had built inside me. So now I am able to eat dinner with the group when Brian is present. I've let go of my angry feelings toward him.

By calming down and allowing for the passage of time, Maureen was able to use her Ladder of Assumptions with respect to Brian to more objectively examine her conflict with him. She was able to identify facts and see what her assumptions were about him. Even without clarifying her assumptions with him, she came to the realization that he could have offended her without her having caused or deserved his outburst. She saw the possibility that it might not have been about her or her actions. In the end, she was able to stop taking personally what he had said and let go of her hurt and angry feelings toward him.

A Mother-Daughter Conflict

The Ladder of Assumptions is a useful tool for finding out what part you played in a dispute—even if you're the only one confronting the problem. It helped with the woman whose holiday visit with her daughter turned sour, as described at the beginning of this chapter.

In the following account, the mother illustrates how it all began:

> I had been looking forward to spending the Christmas holiday together with Joanie. She arrived from San Jose the afternoon of Christmas Eve. Together we enjoyed an early candlelight service, with caroling and food, to which a friend had invited us. We had also planned, at Joanie's suggestion, to attend a service of lessons and carols at 10:00 p.m. We had done this in past years as a family and also in later years. However, after we returned from the first event, Joanie closeted herself in her room and then said she didn't want to attend the later service. I didn't want to go by myself, so I stayed home.
>
> On Christmas morning, we were invited to have brunch at the home of friends. That afternoon we were going to celebrate in my home with a few women who otherwise didn't have family or friends with whom to celebrate. However, in the morning, Joanie was uncommunicative and was wearing

her street clothes. She asked me when the brunch was to take place. I told her and asked whether she was going to change her clothes. She said she wasn't going to our friends' home and wanted me to take her to the train station so she could return to San Jose.

Joanie had told me she was feeling bad because she couldn't enjoy the holidays with her boyfriend, who lives in another state. Besides that, she told me she wasn't happy about her job because she disliked a lot about her boss. However, I felt she was being selfish and thinking only of her own feelings and not at all about mine. I felt my joy had been taken from me. While I was washing dishes, I was crying, which I thought she could hear.

Later, when I took her to the train station, even though I felt angry, upset, and resentful, I didn't say anything about my feelings.

The woman later created in her mind a Ladder of Assumptions about the situation. These were the rungs of her Ladder:

- The **setting** was my home.

- The **facts** were that my daughter and I had made plans for celebrating Christmas Eve and Christmas Day together. These included attending a service of lessons and carols, visiting friends, and hosting friends at my home. My daughter did not participate in any of these events and instead returned to her apartment in San Jose.

- I **interpreted** my daughter's behavior as thoughtless, selfish, and uncaring.

- The **motives** I attributed to my daughter were that she wanted to withdraw because she was so upset, hurt, and angry. She didn't care about me or whether her actions had a negative impact on me.

- I **stereotyped** her as one of the younger generation who is thoughtless. I felt they consider only their own self-interest and not that of others.

- My **actions** were that I didn't speak with her and decided to wait to see if she would explain her actions to me.

Later, the woman told us, she calmed down and decided to make the most of the day. "I had a good time at my friends' home as well as later on at my own party, where we all shared a warm, wonderful feeling and holiday spirit."

The positive experiences helped her to step down her Ladder of Assumptions. This gave her the space to recognize that her daughter's behavior wasn't about her at all. Her daughter was wrapped up in her own feelings of hurt about her boyfriend and disappointment with her boss.

In this case, the Ladder of Assumptions helped the mother differentiate the facts from her assumptions and find peace after a troubling emotional ride. "Stepping down" a Ladder doesn't necessarily mean revisiting each rung. It means stepping back down to the factual level and examining in your own mind what actually had happened.

Even without talking with her daughter about what had taken place, the mother realized her daughter hadn't done anything to try to intentionally upset or hurt her. The daughter had acted out of her own unhappy feelings, which had nothing to do with her mother. Her daughter hadn't apologized, but the mother was able to move on all the same.

A Daughter-Father Conflict

In the case above, the mother went through the Ladder of Assumptions without her daughter because she chose to handle the conflict alone. There are times, however, when the person with unresolved feelings has no other choice. Glenda talked with one of us about negative feelings she had had toward her father most of her life. Her father had long since died, but Glenda still wished to confront the longstanding grudge she had held against him.

Glenda wrote this account on her ninety-seventh birthday:

> During my early years, it seemed ours was a happy family. I never heard my parents quarrel. And so it came as quite a shock when my mother told me and my younger sister that our father was no longer going to live with us.
>
> When my parents divorced, I was thirteen years old and my sister was eleven. News of the divorce was published in the local paper. My sister and I felt embarrassed and ashamed when our school friends told us they had read in the newspaper about our family splitting up.
>
> Under the terms of the divorce settlement, my sister and I were to receive child-support payments until we reached eighteen years of age. That is exactly what happened. Our father stopped our child support payments when we reached that age. But at the age of eighteen, we still were his daughters and still needed the money he had been giving us to pay for our school expenses. We felt abandoned by him, as if he had thrown us away.

This is the Ladder of Assumptions I created in my mind about our father:

- The **setting** was our home.

- The **facts** were that I became eighteen, and I no longer received child-support payments from my father.

- I **interpreted** my father's behavior as heartless and selfish.

- The **motives** I attributed to my father were that he no longer loved me and was glad he didn't have to make my child-support payments any longer.

- I **stereotyped** him as a "deadbeat dad."

- My **actions** were that I was no longer loving toward him, and I carried a lifelong grudge toward him.

Now, on my ninety-seventh birthday, I have finally reached a decision to go back down my original Ladder of Assumptions, let go of my bitter feelings toward my father, and forgive him. Looking back almost eighty years later, I now realize my father was a good father to us, not heartless and selfish. After the divorce was final, he showed he was loving toward us by making every one of his required child support payments. I'm sure he felt he was being a good father, not a "deadbeat dad." If I had gone to him after my eighteenth birthday and asked for some additional financial help, I now believe he probably would have made every effort to help me.

For most of her life, Glenda had held her father responsible for financial problems she had had as a young woman, which kept her tied to the past. Even though her father had died long before, writing this account gave Glenda an opportunity to release him of that responsibility and to express her gratitude to him. Letting go of an old hurt toward the end of her life enabled her to finally forgive him and be at peace with him.

Finishing the old business Glenda had carried with her for much of her life opened a door to a new level of understanding about her father and a deeper level of calm within herself. Eight days after she wrote this account, she suffered a stroke. Two days later, she died peacefully in her sleep.

When you gather together all the people involved in a dispute, you can get a better sense of everyone's assumptions. But sometimes that isn't possible. The experiences of Glenda, the mother who felt jilted by her daughter, and Maureen demonstrate how, even without any of the others coming to the table with you, you can find a way to resolve conflicts by yourself.

Concluding Tips

Know that interpersonal conflicts can be resolved, even if one party to the conflict is unwilling to cooperate or is unavailable.

1. Take responsibility for any Ladder of Assumptions you create about another person. You have total control over what you decide to do with Ladders of Assumptions that you make about others.

2. Calm yourself by considering each of the rungs of any Ladder of Assumptions you create.[12] Dispassionately reexamine your conflict. Reflect on the way in which your assumptions may have caused the negative feelings you have experienced.

3. Allow the feelings generated by any Ladder of Assumptions you build about another person to diffuse and ultimately fade away. Make deliberate decisions to let go of each feeling about another person that your own assumptions have caused.

---

12 Although we ask that you consider each rung, it's not the case that every rung is reached when one races up a Ladder of Assumptions. For instance, a stereotype or sweeping generalization might not have come into play.

Figure out for yourself how to not take another person's behavior personally.

1. Understand that a person's behavior toward you may be caused by a number of factors, and the other person may be unaware of any or all of them. People respond to you based on things that are happening in their own lives. Other factors may be heredity, early life conditioning, cultural factors, and, sometimes, traumatic experiences.

2. Become aware that you may have been a trigger for another person's reactions to you. You do not cause another person's behavior; rather, the assumptions the person makes about you causes his or her own behavior.

3. State to yourself, "I don't have to take his behavior personally," whenever a person is reacting to you in a manner you judge to be negative. Rely on this self-help tool to avoid racing up a Ladder of Assumptions about another person's negative behavior toward you.

Activities

Reflect on a conflict you may be having with someone who is unwilling to discuss the conflict with you or is unavailable to do so.

Write down the following:

- a Ladder of Assumptions you have built about the person and

- the feelings your assumptions have caused you to have.

Are you able to release any negative feelings that your Ladder of Assumptions caused you to have?

If it is possible to reconnect with the person, write down the action steps you will take. For a personal account that shows how a woman took steps to contact her brother after having been estranged from him for four years, read Appendix IV.

CHAPTER 7

MOVING FORWARD

You must be the change you want to see in the world.

—Mahatma Gandhi

One night at dinner at her son's home, Betty had a fight with her daughter-in-law. They raised their voices at each other, and the daughter-in-law threw Betty out. That began a long period when the two women weren't talking, and Betty felt cut off from her grandchildren's lives. Throughout that time, Betty felt as if she were carrying a weight within her. We will come back to Betty's conflict with her daughter-in-law later in this chapter.

The burden of an unresolved conflict is a lot like carrying a toddler around or hauling a school backpack. When you put the toddler down or finally drop your books on your desk, your first few steps feel as if you are as light as a feather. Pounds lighter, you feel relieved and liberated.

In the same way, after you take steps to resolve the conflict, you may experience a state of relief. As time moves you further away from the conflict, you may feel the conflict is genuinely resolved, with no or few lingering feelings of remorse, anger, or hurt.

However, even if everyone involved in a conflict agrees to set aside false assumptions and meet on common ground, the relationship can still feel tenuous. You may wonder where you go from here. How do you begin to repair bruised emotions? How do you restore the relationship?

Bank of Goodwill and Trust

Turning around a conflict usually takes time. It requires a recognizable and sustained change of behavior. With this book, you've learned the actions that constitute "investments" in a bank of goodwill and trust:

- understanding our minds
- becoming self-aware
- listening for understanding
- clarifying assumptions
- communicating constructively
- reaching agreements

The goal is to ensure the investments and savings in your bank of goodwill are greater than the withdrawals that diminish the account.

Once you understand the main reasons for your disagreement, you can begin to move forward by steadily investing and saving—by honoring the agreements you've made. But there will no doubt be occasional "withdrawals" that will accompany the "deposits." Not honoring the spirit of an agreement constitutes a withdrawal. Deposits can be in the form of subsequent discussions requiring good listening skills, letting go of blame, a willingness to work through emotions (perhaps privately), and working together to find a satisfying resolution.

Every time a person honors an agreement, that individual is building trust. You can see how the concept of a bank of goodwill and trust works when you look back at the agreement Rob and Ann worked out in chapter 5.

Ann's Hours

Ann's job dictated that on many nights she had to work into the late evening. Rob's job was just the opposite. You could set your watch by the time Rob arrived home. In a proposed agreement between Rob and Ann, Ann suggested she would try to return home from work at a reasonable hour.

Every work day that Ann called to say she was leaving work and came home before 7:30, she was investing in their relationship, making a deposit in her bank of goodwill and trust. When she wasn't home by 7:30 and also hadn't called, she made a withdrawal. When trust is low, it might be a big deal to Rob if Ann shows up even two minutes past their agreed time. Imagine how he might feel, however, if Ann came home at 7:32 after she had honored her agreement for a whole month. Rob might not have even noticed that she arrived two minutes later than she said she would.

Building Trust

Trust is built by consistent behavior change, and moving forward requires a belief that the changes both parties are making can last. To increase the likelihood of your agreement lasting, consider how you might support each other to make the desired changes. Include those supporting roles in your final agreement. For example, you might want to be reminded of a particular behavior through the use of a word, phrase, or action you both agree on.

Whether you can ever resolve a conflict with another person depends on many factors.

- How motivated is each person involved in the conflict? The person who is least motivated can limit if and when the conflict will be left behind for good.

- How much emotional damage has been experienced? Emotions from a conflict stemming from a one-time, flippant comment by a coworker at a meeting is different from finding out ten years into marriage that your spouse had been having an affair from year two.

- What are the positive possibilities and opportunities for you?

- What are the risks of doing something versus doing nothing and "letting sleeping dogs lie"?

- How does the other person benefit from resolving the conflict?

- If the other person in the conflict resists your overtures to resolve the problem, what might you be able to do that would make that person receptive?

- If the other person in the conflict does not become receptive, what can you do for yourself to make it easier for you to live with the unresolved issue (as modeled in the accounts in chapter 6)?

Complicating matters, you may berate yourself for your own contribution to what was hurtful to the other person. You may feel guilt and shame over what you said or did. Being able to forgive oneself for past feelings and actions is important because when we hold on to self-critical judgments, we take ourselves out of the present. We carry this self-diminishing emotional baggage into current interactions with the other person in the conflict, which inhibits us from being our true selves when relating to that person.

Regardless of the other person's willingness to address a

conflict, you can start each day with a strong foundation of honoring yourself and maintain that attitude throughout the day.

Here are some examples of actions you can take that might be helpful for you:

1. Write down things you can try that might ease the conflict.

2. Begin your day with thoughts of behaving in these new ways as you go about your daily life—while doing such things as dressing or going to work. Remind yourself that you really are a good person and want to demonstrate that to others.

3. Anticipate that you may encounter conflicts many times during the day, but affirm you can deal with them in a positive way.

4. If you want to, share with another person you trust what you intend to do. Support always helps.

5. Be serious about your intent, but add a little laughter and humor to each day.

6. Remember that the past is the past and we can learn from it, but it is over. We live in the present and look forward to learning and living in a new way.

7. Write a letter to yourself, acknowledging the new behaviors you've tried that day.

8. Compliment yourself when you have moved, even in very small ways, toward accomplishing a behavioral goal.

One Conflict, Several Possible Outcomes

Conflicts and their resolutions are not one-size-fits-all. Each conflict is unique, and its resolution depends on the needs of the individuals involved. The conflict between Betty and her daughter-in-law, which we described at the beginning of this chapter, could have a variety of different outcomes, many of which would leave Betty able to move on with her life. We'll take a look at how the conflict may have played out. First, Betty will tell in detail what happened:

> My daughter-in-law, Janet, and my son, Ted, have two children: Troy, from Janet's earlier relationship, and Sam, their own child. Sam is eight years younger than Troy. From things I've directly and indirectly heard, Janet has always felt I favor Sam. One example Janet has brought up is that I've gone to watch many of Sam's soccer games, but I've rarely gone to any of Troy's games.
>
> One night while I was having dinner at their house, conversation themes revolved

around lack of time, given both parents' busy work schedules and their juggling all the family members' after-school and work activities. Trying to help, I offered various solutions, including questioning whether they both really had to work. In hindsight, I realize my suggestions might have come across as veiled criticisms, because Janet was getting increasingly agitated, probably feeling personally criticized and judged by me.

Not one to keep her feelings inside, Janet had clearly had enough of the conversation topics. She yelled at me, accusing me of blindness to Ted's imperfections and favoritism toward Sam. I realized she considered my suggestions personal insults. I was caught completely off-guard. I felt attacked, and I defended myself. I raised my voice and threw a few sarcastic retorts at her. The outcome of this argument was that Janet told me not to contact her or her children. Ted immediately drove me home. He seemed forlorn and caught between two strongly opinionated women.

To reflect on the situation, I wrote down my Ladder of Assumptions:

- The **setting** was my son and daughter-in-law's house where the three of us were eating dinner together.

- The **facts** were that Ted, Janet, and I talked about their lack of time together because of their respective work schedules and their parental roles with regard to their sons' after-school activities. I asked if they both had to work. Janet described her feelings about my relationships with Ted and their sons.

- I **interpreted** Janet's behavior as defensive, strongly opinionated, and judgmental.

- The **motive** I attributed to Janet was that she wanted to punish me by forbidding me to contact her or my grandchildren.

- I **stereotyped** her as a typical daughter-in-law who believes mothers-in-law are critical of their daughters-in-law and favor their sons.

- My **actions** were that I responded to Janet by raising my voice and directing sarcastic remarks at her.

So how might this conflict play out? Here are scenarios that illustrate three different ways in which the family members in this dispute might "move forward":

Scenario 1: One side is willing to talk; the other avoids the conflict.

Scenario 2: One side dies before the conflict is addressed.

Scenario 3: Both sides are willing to resolve the conflict.

From Betty's point of view, here's how each scenario would play out:

Scenario 1: One side is willing to talk; the other avoids the conflict

> At first, I stayed at the top of my Ladder of Assumptions. I was furious, feeling incorrectly characterized and unfairly punished in a cruel manner. I wasn't even allowed to talk to Janet to find out exactly what she was mad about. I absolutely could not understand her, and I wasn't going to grovel or apologize for something I hadn't done. I couldn't get past the fact that she was depriving me of any contact with my grandsons. I was their grandmother, and I felt I had the right to express my love to them.
>
> In the immediate aftermath, I tried to ask

Ted my questions but often found myself getting angry at him for not doing something about Janet and shaking sense into her. Ted finally got angry at me and began avoiding me.

For two years, I never went to my son's home and had little contact with my grandsons. Janet and Ted's family stopped spending Christmas with the extended family. The four of them celebrated alone.

My anger eventually morphed into resignation. My need for answers and understanding seemed to lessen, and I became willing to accept my relationship on Janet's terms. I did a lot of self-reflecting over time and started coming back down my Ladder of Assumptions, acknowledging unfounded assumptions I had made. I realized I did favor Sam a little over Troy. Troy was already eight years old when I first met him, and it took time for me to get to know him. I already loved Sam from when Janet was pregnant with him. I was able to be part of his life from the very beginning. But I know in my heart that I always did my best to treat both my grandsons with the love I felt for each.

Janet and Ted were married eight years after they first met. Both their kids were turning out fine. They were doing decently in school; they had friends; they were involved in sports; and they were staying out of trouble. These facts helped me to eventually see that Janet and Ted were living their lives the way they decided was best for their family. I forgave Janet. Without any ill will toward her, I accepted that I might not ever see her or my grandsons again, although I desperately did not want that to be the case. Equally hard as forgiving her was forgiving myself for my own "bad" behaviors (yelling back, blaming, trying to convince others to change).

Gradually, the feud thawed. Ted would occasionally come to my house on special occasions, but conversations were strained. As more time passed, Ted occasionally brought Sam along with him. Through this occasional contact, I was able to keep up with what was going on with the family, even though I wasn't an active participant. In time, I invited the family to my house for dinner, and they accepted. We stuck to safe topics of conversation to avoid ruffling feathers. Later, I was invited to Janet and Ted's house.

The more visits we had, the more we were able to behave like our natural selves.

I've never asked Janet to tell her side of the story and tell me whether my guesses about why she cut off communication were accurate. And she hasn't discussed it. If she brings it up, I'm willing to discuss it. But for myself and my needs, I'm okay with what I have now. I don't feel as though I'm walking on eggshells or avoiding landmines. I just am who I am, and I suppose I've changed, having gone through this. Even though there are still some unanswered questions, my gratefulness to have the family back overshadows any unease. I think the internal work I've done while we were out of communication has allowed me to accept them as they are, and I can simply be present, not living in the past. I don't know what will come in the future, but I will respond then as best I can.

In this example, the conflict didn't get resolved by Janet and Betty. They didn't listen to each other, discuss what the "conflict" was, check out assumptions, or apologize. They seem to be avoiding rather than resolving conflict.

However, it's worth taking a look at what Betty did that played a part in turning around the conflict. Betty reflected internally on her own perspectives, attitudes, and actions, regardless of what Janet was doing. She examined her contributions—her thoughts and attitudes—to the conflict. She seemed to let go of her assumptions about what had caused Janet's actions. She accepted that she, too, had behaved badly and eventually was able to come to terms with that, rather than beat herself up or dwell on it.

By not dwelling on the past, worrying, or feeling defensive, Betty feels she'll be able to listen, be honest, and be compassionate. Until one of the participants decides to actively pursue resolution, the conflict may either dissolve or, because of the emotional baggage Janet may still be carrying, even escalate.

Scenario 2: One side dies before the conflict is addressed

Imagine if Janet had died during the time she and Betty were estranged. The same type of internal work Betty did in Scenario 1 would probably have given Betty acceptance and peace.

There are times it is effective to forgive, even though an offender has not offered an explanation or extended an apology. This is especially true when the person committing the perceived offense has died. (See Glenda's story in chapter 6 for an example.)

Some people have already made up their minds they will

never release their offender from old hurts and instead hold grudges and resentments that can last a lifetime. But some of humanity's wisest visionaries agree that letting go of old wounds is important for the well being of everyone who is involved in interpersonal strife.

Frederic Luskin is director of the Stanford (University) Forgiveness Project. In 2001, he and six colleagues conducted a study on 259 adults who had at least one unresolved "hurtful" experience that left them with what Luskin called "negative" results. The study was subsequently published in the *Journal of Clinical Psychology*. The study found that people could be trained to forgive, and that in forgiving people, the participants relieved their stress.[13] In *Forgive for Good*, the book Luskin wrote about the study, he offers a nine-step method for forgiving that, he says, makes it possible to move beyond being a victim.

Luskin stresses that forgiving another person is not the equivalent of condoning that person's behavior or ignoring the hurtful events that had occurred. On the contrary, it involves setting aside your pain and anger, and not holding someone else (including someone who has died)

---

13 "Forgive for Good" at Learningtoforgive.com, "Effects of Group Forgiveness Intervention on Perceived Stress, State and Trait, Anger, Symptoms of Stress, Self-Reported Health and Forgiveness (Stanford Forgiveness Project)," accessed February 24, 2012. http://learningtoforgive.com/research/effects-of-group-forgiveness-intervention-on-perceived-stress-state-and-trait-anger-symptoms-of-stress-self-reported-health-and-forgiveness-stanford-forgiveness-project/.

responsible for your emotional well being.[14] Forgiveness allows you to move on.

Scenario 3: Both sides are willing to resolve the conflict

As Betty recalls:

> At first, I was furious, feeling unjustly and incorrectly characterized and unfairly punished in a cruel manner. I wasn't allowed to talk to Janet to find out exactly what she was mad about. I could absolutely not understand her, and I wasn't going to grovel or apologize for I didn't know what. And how could she deprive me of any contact with my grandsons? I'm their grandmother, and I have the right to express my love to them.
>
> In the immediate aftermath, I attempted to ask Ted to help me understand why Janet was so angry but often found myself getting angry at him for not doing something about our predicament. Ted would listen to my questions and acknowledge how painful the situation was for me. He said he wanted to support me but that this issue was really between me and Janet, and he couldn't

---

14 Frederic Luskin, *Forgive For Good* (New York: HarperCollins Publishers, Inc., 2001).

answer for Janet. He kept reminding me that I was probably displacing my frustration over the situation with anger toward him. We talked over some ideas of what might be effective ways to directly communicate with Janet and in what time frame.

I waited a few weeks and then I sent Janet a letter. I tried to show in what I wrote that I had let go of my negative assumptions about her and that I now saw her in a different light. It was brief. I essentially just shared the fact that first and foremost, I loved her. I apologized for the hurtful things I said to her at dinner that night.

I told her I felt horrible that the evening's conversation, particularly what I said, had upset her so much. I suggested that if she was up to it, whenever that might be, I would like to go for a walk with her and just talk things out.

Months later, Janet called suggesting we go for that walk. It ended up being a long one, where we talked honestly and openly like never before. After we had built enough comfort and trust, I shared with her that I had realized I did favor Sam a little over Troy and why that was. I told her I couldn't imagine my life without Troy, and I shared some specific memories involving him and me.

We didn't formalize any "agreements," but we did talk about doing things differently in the future. We encouraged each other and gave each other permission to talk about whatever might be bothering her or me. We both felt we had the tendency to bottle up tensions. We knew we both tended to talk to Ted about our issues with each other, rather than talking directly with each other. We said we'd try really hard to not put Ted in the middle. We agreed that no matter how mad we were at each other, we were a family, and not talking was not a solution.

No conflict follows a specific template. Just as Betty's conflict with her daughter-in-law might have gone in three different directions, your conflicts can take different turns. Examine the facts of the conflicts and the assumptions you made, and be willing to forgive and move on.

When you reflect on a situation in which you are experiencing a conflict with someone, you may want to assess how you feel in relation to the other person and how she feels about you. Create a Ladder of Assumptions for each of you, drawing on the steps outlined in Appendix V. In yours, list the assumptions you made about the other person. In hers, record the assumptions you think she would have made about you, including these elements:

- her understanding of the setting
- her sense of the facts
- her interpretation of your behavior
- her guess as to your motives
- her sense of the stereotypes she may have been drawing on
- her actions that stemmed from her assumptions

This is the time to clarify with her the assumptions you made in these two Ladders. Now that you've created a Ladder of what you think her assumptions were about you, ask if she'd be willing to talk with you about this Ladder. If she is willing, ask her to verify these assumptions and correct those with which she disagrees.

Now it's time to ask her to look at the Ladder you've created about her behavior and ask her to verify and correct these assumptions. Continue this process until you both agree on the assumptions that are valid on both Ladders.

After this, check in with yourself from time to time to gauge how much you have let go of your negative assumptions and feelings toward her.

Here is a step-by-step process for checking in with yourself:

- Reflect on the stories or accounts you might share

with people about difficult events or periods you have had with the woman.

- Ask yourself, when you are discussing the conflict with another person, "am I characterizing her in even mildly negative terms." If so, it is a reminder that you still have some lingering hurt feelings.

- Try to have compassion for yourself.

- Write what you can do to help release your unfounded assumptions and negative feelings of having been injured by her.

Hopefully she would be willing to carry out a self-reflection process concerning any lingering assumptions and negative feelings she may have, similar to the process you are following.

Make agreements about how you will behave toward each other in the future, including commitments to avoid the offensive behavior of the past.[15] Acknowledge that, despite these agreements, each of you will continue to look at the world from somewhat different angles. Just because you're able to turn the corner on your conflict does not mean the two of you have been transformed into perfect people.

Even though you may both be moving forward, events may arise that again provoke frustration and irritation,

---

15 See chapter 5 on developing agreements.

if not anger. Conflicts may still occur, which means that on such occasions, the two of you will need to once again put into practice the skills covered in this book: clarifying assumptions, apologizing for those that proved to be unfounded, accepting those you both agreed to, and starting over once again.

Now, for a moment, let's return to the ending in **Scenario 3: Both sides are willing to resolve the conflict** in this chapter. What if Betty and Janet hadn't been able to resolve their differences in the manner described in this scenario and were facing a future of permanent estrangement. Might there still have been hope for them? Read the next chapter to learn about an option—mediation—that they could have pursued.

Concluding Tips

Commit to putting conflicts behind you and moving forward.

1. Be truly interested in reconciling with the other person in the conflict. Be willing to move forward without holding grudges.

2. Acknowledge that a full-fledged effort on your part is required to change old habits. Take small, doable steps that move you closer to changing old habits, and record them after you've accomplished them.

3. Expect the best from the other person, giving her the benefit of the doubt if an issue arises. Avoid the inclination to second-guess the behavior of the other person.

Make adjustments when necessary.

1. Be willing to acknowledge to the other person in the conflict when you have faltered in your behavior. Apologize if you have not upheld your commitment to change.

2. If the other person has not upheld his commitment to change, accept his apology. Make your best effort to be magnanimous.

3. You and the other person should commit to identifying and agreeing upon needed changes in your behavior. Acknowledge to yourself and the other person that things don't always work out as planned.

Activities

1. Recall a time when you were able to resolve a challenging conflict and felt good about the outcome.

2. Write the Ladder of Assumptions you formed about the other person.

3. Write what you think the other person's Ladder of Assumptions was about you.

4. Tell how you came down your Ladder and why you were able to do it.

5. Tell how the other person came down his Ladder and why he was able to do it.

6. Describe the outcome.

7. Explain what made the outcome possible.

8. Describe the contribution you made to the resolution of the conflict.

9. Summarize what you learned from the experience.

CHAPTER 8

MEDIATION

Peace is not the absence of conflict but the presence of creative alternatives for responding to conflict.

—Dorothy Thompson

A middle-aged woman is worried that her father, hundreds of miles away, is living all alone. She would like him to sell his house and move to a senior-living community, where she knows he will be cared for. The father has built memories over the previous four decades and doesn't want to leave his neighbors and friends.

The two have been talking past each other for some time without coming close to resolving their conflict. They have become so polarized they are barely speaking to each other. When they do talk, their conversation typically deteriorates almost immediately into a shouting match. Neither is willing to acknowledge the other has anything valid to say. Even sharing their Ladders of Assumptions is totally out of the question.

The end to the deadlock comes through mediation.

There are times it seems nothing will help you settle your differences. And it may be that even with the best intentions and concerted efforts to apply what you learn within these pages, you face disputes that appear to be intractable.

There is still hope. We all became mediators because we saw how an independent third party could help break down the seemingly solid walls between people.

A mediator is a third party who is not involved in the conflict. The mediator does not decide who is right or wrong and, in fact, does not recommend a decision of any kind. It is the mediator's job to ensure that each disputant is fully heard and that everyone has an opportunity to express his or her real needs.

Ground rules in mediations keep disputants from throwing angry language at each other, and the mediator makes sure those rules are followed.

If there is one fear that keeps many people from coming to the mediation table, it is the fear of sitting across from your adversary one more time and getting a lot of angry words thrown at you with no hope of getting beyond them.

Mediation involves two or more people who haven't been able to agree on a solution to their problem plus a mediator, who has no stake in the outcome of the mediation. The mediation process allows people to express their feelings, clarify their assumptions about each other, clear up misunderstandings and find areas of agreement that can be incorporated into solutions that the people themselves create.

Here's what happens in the mediation with the father and daughter. The session takes place in a room at the mediator's office.

Anna Steele, the mediator, is at the head of the table. To her left is Harold Greene, the widower, slumped in his chair, obviously ill at ease. Tanya Ellison, Harold's married daughter, sits across from her father, appearing worried and fidgeting with her hands in her lap. Here's how the session goes:

> **Anna**: One of the reasons I'm here is to help you talk with one another about issues you have found difficult to discuss. I will not take sides, nor will I let things get out of hand. After you have talked and listened to each other and have considered and discussed options for resolving your differences, I will try to help you work out an agreement. You may not be able to reach an agreement at this first meeting, which is all right. But hopefully you will.
>
> **Tanya**: I'm terribly upset because Dad just won't listen to me and realize he's got to do

something about his living arrangements. I love him dearly and know he simply can't continue to live at home alone any longer. He gets dizzy sometimes; he doesn't take his medications when he should; and he doesn't eat the proper food. I'm awfully afraid that he may fall and hurt himself and no one will be there to help him. Living six hundred miles away, I certainly can't be there when he might need me.

Harold: I don't know what Tanya's talking about. She talks like I'm nothing but a used-up old man. The truth is, I'm fit as a fiddle. I drive my car, and I get out for walks three times a day. Just ask my neighbors. They'll tell you how spry I am. And when I need something, they're the first ones to help me. We've known each other for more than forty years, and we trust each other because we've been through a lot of hard times together. The only way I'm leaving my home is when they carry me out feet first.

Tanya: I know Dad has a lot of friends in his neighborhood, but they're getting old, just as he is. And they're not going to be able to live there indefinitely either. Ever since Mom died ten years ago, Dad has hung on to the house for dear life because that's where the two of them raised their family, and it has lots of memories for him. But he won't give any thought at all as to whether it's the wisest course for him now. He thinks he doesn't have any options. But he does.

And I forgot to point out that Dad's home is falling apart on him. The repairs on the house, which he used to be able to do, he just can't anymore, and he refuses to hire contractors to do the work for him. The house is sixty years old and is really a mess. It needs new wallpaper and paint. He sure can't do it by himself, and he can't expect his neighbors to do it for him.

Harold: All this nonsense about me not keeping my house up and needing to move into a retirement home ...

I don't want to be around old people using walkers and wheeling around in wheelchairs. Besides, if I moved into a retirement home, all my longtime friends and relatives would forget about me. I'm not what you'd call a social person. It takes me a long time to open up with people and trust them enough for us to become friends.

Tanya: Dad just isn't being realistic. There are all kinds of activities and social programs at senior-living facilities that are designed to help the people living there get better acquainted. People don't become good friends instantly, but you can't expect that. When they see each other day after day, they become friendly soon enough. Dad would do just fine at one of these places, but he just won't admit it. Besides, he needs to live someplace where he can get three meals a day and where someone can make sure he takes his medications.

Harold: Even if I did get to know a few people after a while, where would I get the money to buy into a retirement home? Where could I go and live as cheaply as I live now? I hear retirement homes are really expensive. Most require a big payment before you ever set foot in your apartment. I just don't have that kind of money. I suppose I could come up with the money to pay the entry fee by selling my house, but there would be big monthly payments after that. With my Social Security check, I barely make ends meet now as it is. It wouldn't be long before I would be out of money.

At the conclusion of the first mediation session, Anna gives Harold and Tanya an assignment. They are to go home, write down the Ladder of Assumptions each has raced up judging the behavior of the other, and return to the next session with their respective Ladders in mind. The Ladder, she explains, represents how we rush to judgment about others and how this causes conflicts.

Tanya and Harold agree, and Tanya drives her father back home. That evening, after her father has gone to bed, Tanya writes the following Ladder of Assumptions about her dad:

- The **setting** is our sixty-year-old family home, where I am visiting my eighty-five-year-old father.

- The **facts** are that I am my father's fifty-six-year-old daughter; I live six hundred miles from his home; and I visit him about every six weeks. Most of our discussions on this visit have been about his living circumstances.

- I **interpreted** Dad as stubborn.

- The **motive** I attributed to Dad is that he doesn't want to face reality about the stage of life he is in.

- I **stereotyped** Dad as one of those old people who are afraid of change and never listen to his kids.

- My **actions** were that I could see nothing in what

Dad said that made any sense, and so I was cold toward him and short-tempered in what I said to him.

Harold doesn't write his assumptions down, but he does compose them in his head. Here are the assumptions he makes about Tanya:

- The **setting** is the sixty-year-old house that my wife and I built several years after we were married and where we raised our family of four kids.

- The **facts** are that my daughter Tanya is visiting me from her home six hundred miles to the east and she is talking with me about my living conditions and giving me her views on that subject.

- I **interpreted** Tanya's comments as wrong because she lives very far away and can't possibly see that I'm doing just fine and taking care of everything.

- The **motive** I attributed to Tanya is that she doesn't really care about what I want to do with my life. If she can convince me to sell my home and move into a senior-living facility, she simply won't have to worry about me anymore.

- I **stereotyped** Tanya as one of those kids who are too big for their britches, dismiss their parents' views, and think their perspectives are the only right ones.

- My **actions** were to let Tanya's comments go in one ear and out the other and keep on doing what I've always been doing.

At the next mediation session, Anna encourages Tanya and Harold to share their Ladders of Assumptions and continue expressing their specific issues, concerns, and feelings. Eventually, they reach the point where they feel they have said everything they wanted to say.

Anna then summarizes what she has heard from Harold and Tanya. The two find that talking to a mediator who has listened with an accepting, empathetic, and nonjudgmental stance has enabled them to finally feel fully heard and to better understand both sides of their disagreement.

In the next phase of the mediation, Anna asks Tanya and Harold to speak directly to each other, restating his or her understanding of the other's point of view. This phase continues until they both agree that each one has fully understood the other's concerns. It has enabled each of them to understand the disagreement from the other's perspective and ultimately take responsibility for their own part in the dispute.

As a result of the exercise, Harold says he really didn't know what it would be like to live in a senior-living facility. He has never seen one. He agrees to have Tanya drive him to a number of nearby facilities so he can check them out firsthand.

Tanya offers to talk with her father's friends and neighbors and encourage them to visit him if he should decide to move from his home. She has also agreed that she and her husband would visit him regularly, and Tanya assures her father that her sister and brothers would do so too. In addition, she promises to encourage her adult children—Harold's grandchildren—to visit him.

Harold comments that a friend his age has hired a caregiver from a business in town and that this has allowed the man to stay in his home. Harold asks Tanya if she could find out more about that business and how much it would cost for him to hire a caregiver. If he could afford to pay someone to shop for groceries, do some cooking, run a few errands, and check on whether he is taking his medications, he might be able to keep living at home for a while longer.

Tanya says she would be glad to look into that business and possibly some others. She also says that if they could find a caregiver they all trust, she and her sister and brothers could probably chip in toward the expense.

At the end of the second session, after Harold and Tanya together have considered a variety of options, the two sign a form listing their agreements. They end the meeting with a warm embrace and walk away arm in arm, to share dinner at a nearby restaurant.

Through mediation, Tanya and Harold have been able to examine the negative labels they had placed on each other and acknowledge the extent to which they had misjudged each other. The process has allowed them to get past the misconceptions to deal with their real interests and eventually move from only talking at each other about problems to devising some mutually acceptable solutions.

If you find yourself facing a seemingly insurmountable disagreement with someone, follow the steps in this book. But know that if you're still not able to work it out, mediation is always an option.

Concluding Tips

This book teaches communication skills that enable you to do the following:

1. Talk through frictions with others before they become out-and-out conflicts.

2. Defuse conflicts that may occur despite your best efforts to head them off.

3. Resolve conflicts through the mediation process, if they persist after you have done all you can on your own to defuse them.

Mediation, as a conflict-resolution process, has distinctive features.

1. The participants are a mediator and two or more

people who haven't been able to get beyond arguments to work out a solution to their conflict.

2. Mediation offers an accepting space where people can give their accounts and share their frustrations to a professional whom they can trust.

    -   The mediator is a professional who is a neutral party, who has no stake in the outcome of the mediation, and who doesn't take sides in the dispute.

    -   The goal of a mediator is to foster a fair environment that facilitates mutual, respectful problem-solving efforts by the parties involved in the conflict.

    -   To reach that goal, a mediator assists the parties to try to communicate clearly with each other. She uses a structured communication process to help them identify their own needs and to work together to develop solutions that meet those needs.

Activity

To obtain further information about the mediation process, we strongly recommend you read Christina Sabee's book, *Mediation: Transforming conflict through communication*, which is listed in the **REFERENCES** section.

CHAPTER 9

WRAPPING UP

Ambiguity, contradictions, uncertainty, even error: to be comfortable with them is the beginning of wisdom.

—Sherwin B. Nuland

Lessons from *Conflict—The Unexpected Gift*

Our purpose in writing this book is to teach you the same practical approach we have taught others experiencing interpersonal conflicts. It is a method that has helped them creatively tackle tough issues while treating the other people in the conflicts with respect and consideration.

Whether your conflict has dragged on because of ideological differences or you have a brief dispute because of your assumptions about another person's words, glance or tone of voice, the techniques included in this book can guide you to a meaningful resolution.

Here are the ten most important lessons we hope you have learned from this book:

1. **Resolving interpersonal conflicts depends on what is going on in the minds of those in conflict with each other.**

When two people are in conflict, their minds have unconsciously raced up metaphorical Ladders of Assumptions about each other. Unless you understand that, you will have difficulty resolving your conflicts with others. The assumptions of each individual are her own. They often are based on such factors as heredity, early life conditioning, cultural factors, and even traumatic experiences. So you don't need to take personally the behavior caused by another person's erroneous assumptions.

2. **Be aware of how people inwardly rush to judgment about others based on preformed assumptions.**

Make it a daily practice to look within and identify those predispositions you have that can lead to instant judgments about others. Each time you feel the need to be right and make critical judgments, you create seeds of conflict. Judging others and not accepting them the way they are is self-defeating and adds fuel to the fire of disharmony.

3. **Listening for understanding lets others know you have heard them and opens you up to hearing their perspectives on your behavior.**

Key to listening for understanding is a sincere desire to

know what is going on with others. It lets you ask questions you might otherwise not have the courage to ask. And it leaves you more open to responses that otherwise would not have found their way into your awareness.

4. **Asking clarifying questions helps you learn how accurate are the assumptions you've made about people with whom you're in conflict.**

We need to respect the right of others to share their perspectives on our assumptions and not judge their views as being wrong, though they may differ from ours. Their observations of our behavior, as well as of their own, are their honest impressions. Their perspectives hold important clues that can lead to a better understanding of the sources of a conflict.

5. **Agreeing to let go of wrong assumptions both sides have held toward each other opens a door to finding common ground.**

When people in conflict are able to let go of invalid assumptions, they have arrived at a common understanding. This, in turn, lets them embrace the principle that it is more important to resolve conflicts and restore relationships than it is for one person to be right and the other to be wrong.

6. **Apologizing sincerely to people you have wronged based on incorrect assumptions and**

actions shows you have taken responsibility for your behavior.

When it's possible, you should include the four aspects of an effective apology: (1) acknowledging the offensive behavior; (2) explaining your actions; (3) expressing remorse; and (4) making amends. Sincerely apologizing shows that you have chosen to move forward. It demonstrates that you have chosen the future, not the past, as the focus for your interactions with others.

7. **Reaching agreement on constructive ways to communicate in the future can help you avoid possible misunderstandings.**

You need to include in your agreements with others solutions that will benefit you both. Although it is important to stick up for your own suggestions for an agreement to be balanced, it is equally important for you to be willing to yield to the other person's ideas. You each need to be willing to be part of the solution.

8. **Resolving interpersonal conflicts on your own is possible.**

You have everything it takes to resolve conflicts on your own. You can take complete responsibility for the Ladders of Assumptions you make about yourself and about the behavior of another person. You are able to reflect on how your assumptions may have caused your own negative feelings about others. And you can decide to let go of those feelings and start fresh with a positive attitude.

9. **Deciding to bury the hatchet lets you set aside old conflicts that have been resolved and start new, positive chapters in your relationships.**

The challenge is to be 100 percent willing to let go of old grudges and move forward expecting the best possible outcomes in renewed relationships. If others falter, you can be magnanimous in giving them the benefit of the doubt—accepting their apologies and their resolve not to let it happen again. Likewise, you need to apologize to others if you veer from the agreed-upon path.

10. **A mediator can help you and the others involved in a conflict reach a resolution that you've not been able to accomplish on your own.**

A third party, who is not involved in a conflict, can help the parties to the conflict hear and view each other in a fresh way. Clearing up previous miscommunications can lead to a new understanding of each other and result in them working together toward a mutually acceptable resolution.

Concluding Tips

Making these lessons part of your life gives you the tools you need to resolve disputes that have been troubling you.

If after reading this book, however, you feel at a loss and don't have any idea where to start, try this approach:

- Briefly leaf through each chapter for the main ideas.

- Write down the one or two skills you think would be the most difficult to learn and apply in your life.

- Put them in a spot where you can look at them frequently.

- Be open to letting them inspire you, rather than discourage you.

Visualize positive outcomes from your focus on them, and you will be surprised at the results a few small changes you make each day can create.

In time, whatever interpersonal conflict you have, you will be able to use the skills you have learned from this book to approach conflict creatively and live and work peacefully with others. You will be able to focus on two Ladders of Assumptions simultaneously—yours and the other person's—and work together to reach agreement on those assumptions that are factual. You will have overcome limitations that kept you from resolving your differences, and in the process you will have become a more understanding and compassionate person.

We wish you the very best on your road to establishing harmonious relationships!

APPENDICES

APPENDIX I

Dimensions of Listening for Understanding

Here's a chart with the four dimensions of listening for understanding, covered in chapter 3. In it you'll find a short summary of each dimension's purpose, a way to respond in your own words, and examples.

Response	Purpose	How to Do This	Examples
ENCOURAGE	To learn more; to draw the speaker out; to get a fuller account.	Invite the speaker to say more, using open-ended questions that can't be answered with a "yes" or "no."	"Tell me what else happened after that. I'd like to know more. Say a little more about that." "I don't fully understand what you're saying. Tell me how you felt about that."
CLARIFY	To try to fully understand what the speaker is saying.	Ask questions that begin with: how, what, with whom, when, where. Avoid "why." It can put the speaker on the spot.	"What led up to this situation? When did this first become a problem for you?" "Who else was involved?" "How did this affect your work?" "When did you first talk with him about it? How often has this occurred?"
RESTATE	To let the speaker know that you are listening; to check your understanding of what's been said.	Tell the speaker what you have heard in your own words.	"From what you told me, I gather that she speaks to you rudely every time she sees you, and treats you disrespectfully." "You seem to be puzzled and angry at her behavior and want her to stop or to tell you what's wrong."
SUMMARIZE	To pull together key points, perceptions and feelings; review everything said. It's a basis for further discussion.	State the main points the other person made, including issues, ideas and feelings.	"When you had your interview, you found out that this might be a good place to work, but now you wonder whether you have all the necessary qualifications and whether you should take the job."

178

APPENDIX II

The Ladder of Assumptions Reveals the Root Cause of a Man's Problem

The **setting** is a branch bank of a national bank where I have a checking account.

The **facts** are that I went to the ATM of the bank to deposit several checks. I entered my ATM card and my PIN number. No option appeared on the screen allowing me to deposit checks to our checking account. I withdrew my ATM card, reinserted it and reentered my PIN number. Again no option appeared for depositing checks. I withdrew my ATM card, reinserted it and reentered my PIN number a third time. Still no option for depositing checks appeared on the screen. I withdrew my ATM card, walked into the bank grumbling about being victimized by the bank, and stood in line waiting to interact with a bank teller.

I **interpreted** the fact that no option for depositing checks appeared on the ATM screen as indicating that the ATM software was malfunctioning.

The **motive** I attributed to the local branch manager was that he didn't care about his clients not being able to make certain financial transactions and that he was in no hurry to fix the malfunctioning ATM software.

I **stereotyped** the local branch manager as a member of

an arrogant management team of the parent bank, that is primarily interested in maximizing the bank's profits and satisfying their shareholders.

My **actions** were that I stepped forward to the next available bank teller, feeling righteously indignant. I told him that the software in the ATM outside the bank is broken, because I had inserted my ATM card and entered my PIN number but was unable to deposit my checks to our checking account. He responded by saying that he would like to have me speak with the branch manager. He walked away and returned several minutes later with the branch manager. I told the branch manager the same account I had given the bank teller, still feeling righteously indignant. The branch manager said, "Let's walk outside to the ATM so that you can show me the problem." We did so. He asked me to insert my ATM card and enter my PIN number. I did. We looked at the screen. Neither of us could see an option on the screen for depositing checks. He then asked me to withdraw my card, which I did. He asked me if he could look at the card so I gave it to him. He looked at it, gave it back to me and said, "This is your credit card, not your ATM card. That is why you haven't been able to get a check deposit option on the screen."

I felt totally humiliated, and told the bank manager how sorry I was for taking his time. I realized that I had raced up a Ladder of Assumptions that had no basis in fact. I quickly went back down my Ladder of Assumptions. I told the manager that all the assumptions I had made were incorrect—even the assumptions I had made about the facts on the first rung of my Ladder—and that I had blamed the bank for my problem when it actually was my problem. I apologized to the manager for my mistake. I told him that in the future I would make very sure I'd use my ATM card. He graciously accepted my apology, and we shook hands. He went back inside the bank, and I went on my way feeling grateful that the two of us had parted company on good terms.

APPENDIX III

The Ladder of Assumptions Helps a
Man Become More Self-Aware

The **setting** is the home of one of the members in a group of ten men that meets for an hour once a week, starting at 8:00 AM. The host of each meeting is the discussion leader for the meeting. The group has been meeting for nearly 35 years. At a recent meeting, the discussion leader's topic was a magazine article featuring 10 things men need to do to lead a healthy and fulfilling life.

The **facts** are that at about 8:50 AM, I said, "I think what has been missing in our discussion so far is the subject of spiritual growth and what each of us needs to be doing in that regard." The discussion leader said, "That is a perfect segue to my final topic—meditation." He proceeded to lead us in a four-minute meditation. When he finished, I said, "The meditation made me think of a spiritual growth situation that occurred in my life a few days ago, involving an interaction I had with a woman who had lost her husband two days before." Another man said, "That happens all the time at the senior center where I live. People die there on a regular basis." Yet another man said, "Situations like that often come up in my life, too." At about 9:05 AM, I said, "I'd like to share with you how I responded to the woman who had lost her husband." Still another man laughed and said, "There you go again. You're always trying to extend the meeting past our agreed upon time of one hour."

I **interpreted** the comment made by the last speaker as disparaging and insensitive.

The **motives** I attributed to him were that he didn't want the meeting to go beyond the regular ending time, and that he wasn't interested in hearing what I wanted to share—an occurrence in my life that I felt was related to the discussion leader's meditation.

I **stereotyped** him as one of the men in the group who thought it an unbreakable rule that the meetings end sharply at 9:00 AM.

My **actions** were that I felt hurt and instantly became angry. I said, "That's it," got up from my seat, abruptly stomped out of the room and left the house. Later that morning, upon further reflection, I realized that I had raced up a Ladder of Assumptions. I settled down and came back down my Ladder. I sent the following email to the man. "I'm sorry I reacted to your comment this morning the way I did. I felt hurt when you said that I had gone on too long with something I was saying, and then got angry. It's an immature behavior I'm trying to change. My reaction had nothing to do with what you said, and everything to do with my habitual response. I need to be more open in the moment to what others say to me. I apologize for getting angry with you this morning. What you said to me turned out to be very helpful. It enabled me to become aware of an unconscious behavior of mine that I need to change. I'm committed to dropping it."

The man responded to my email later that afternoon: "Thanks for your email. I was going to call you and apologize for hurting your feelings, but you beat me to it. I think you do have a tendency to sometimes unconsciously want to prolong meetings, but none of us, certainly not I, doubts your good intentions."

APPENDIX IV

Anita's Action To Resolve A
Conflict With Her Brother

I was the second child in a farm family of five children. When I was six years old, my parents divorced. They had reached a point where they really hated each other. The court gave custody of the children to my father, who split us up. My older brother went to live with my father. I was sent to live with our only aunt. My mother agreed to take my younger sister, leaving me feeling unloved by my mother. My two younger brothers were sent to live with some other relatives.

In time, my father remarried and we all went to live with him and our new stepmother, who was very loving to all of us. From time to time, I thought about contacting my mother, but I knew it would really upset my father if I did. So, I never followed through with my desire to get in touch with her, even though I did see her once or twice at family weddings. When I did see her, I had no feelings for her because she hadn't been the mother I grew up with. Eventually, all of us kids got married and went our separate ways. Over the years, I had occasional contact with my younger sister and my older brother, and maintained what I felt were good relationships with them.

Four years ago, my mother passed away. She was in her 90s when she died. A day after she died, I learned about her passing from the local undertaker in the small rural town near where we all lived. I felt devastated when I learned about my mother's death from a total stranger and not from my older brother who had kept in close touch with our mother. Here is the Ladder of Assumptions I went up about my brother.

The **setting** was the small rural town where my brother and I lived.

The **facts** were that my older brother had kept in contact with our mother over the years. The day she died, my brother did not call me to tell me that she had passed away.

I **interpreted** my brother's behavior as disrespectful, when he didn't call me the day our mother died. I had always had a good relationship with him, and so I couldn't understand why he hadn't called me. Even though my mother had never been a mother to me, it seemed as though my brother had just tossed me aside when he didn't inform me of my mother's passing.

The **motive** I attributed to my brother was that when he didn't talk with me after our mother died, he was ashamed about not having done the right thing by me. During these years, I would occasionally see my brother and his wife in local stores while we were shopping. He invariably would not look at me and would walk away from me toward another part of the store. My brother simply ignored me, not giving me the common courtesy of acknowledging me. From his point of view, I was an outsider as far as my mother was concerned and probably couldn't have cared less that she had died.

I **stereotyped** my brother as a man who had a hard time owning up to having done something wrong, just like men do. He also probably assumed that I was like other women, who are raised from early childhood by a stepmother—they don't develop a bond with their real mother. As a result, he no doubt concluded that he didn't need to inform me that our mother had died.

My **actions** were that I finally decided after four years that I had had enough of being angry with my brother and estranged from him. I was determined to restore the relationship between us, and I knew that I had to take the bull by the horns if anything were going to change. I picked up the phone and called his home. His wife answered. I told her that I wanted to visit them, so that I could have a talk with my brother. She said that that was fine, and we set a date and time.

When I arrived at their home, both of them greeted me. We sat down and started talking. But, whenever I broached the subject of why my brother hadn't called me the day our mother died, his wife came to his defense and chimed in with reasons from her perspective as to why he hadn't called me.

Finally, feeling frustrated at that point, I looked right at my brother and said that I wanted to hear directly from him why he hadn't called me. He said that our mother had told him he didn't need to contact me, or our two younger brothers, because the three of us had had so little contact with her over the years.

I told my brother that after our mother died, the most important thing for him to have done was not necessarily to have honored her wishes to the letter but rather he should have treated all the surviving children in the right way. After all, I told him, I was our mother's daughter, despite the fact that we had very little contact over the years, and that he should have treated me accordingly. We talked back and forth this way for a while until I saw that he understood why I had been so angry with him.

At that point, I asked him if things were all right between us again. He said they were. Then I said I thought we needed a hug. We both got up from our chairs and gave each other hugs. It felt so good! All of us said goodbye, and I walked away feeling sure that my brother and I had repaired our relationship.

APPENDIX V

Putting Into Practice What You Have Been Learning

Part 1

We occasionally hear from some of our students that they are completely in sync with the approach to resolving conflicts in *Conflict—The Unexpected Gift*, and that they are ready to apply the process in conflicts they are currently having with other people. However, they question whether the process will also work when applying it with a conflict partner who hasn't read our book and who hasn't received our training.

Our response to that question is that it can. We have encouraged the people who have asked the question to try out the process with a conflict partner who hasn't been exposed to it. The purpose is to test whether the process can work in such situations. We acknowledge that the process may not work in every instance.

Here is an outline that you can follow to try out the process with someone with whom you currently are in a conflict and who is unfamiliar with our process. We recommend that you do one part at a time since this is a multi-step activity.

1. Identify a conflict you currently are having with someone, which you and the person have not been

able to resolve and to which you are willing to apply the approach in *Conflict—The Unexpected Gift* to the best of your ability.

2. Commit to the following ground rules:

    *   Be respectful toward your conflict partner.

    *   Be responsible for how you have behaved in the relationship with the other person, and for the assumptions you have made about her.

    *   Be honest with your conflict partner, striving at all times to be authentic and straightforward— avoiding hidden agendas and deceptive maneuvers.

    *   Be open to your conflict partner's comments and feedback, giving full consideration to the validity of what she says.

    *   Be agreeable to arriving at a resolution that benefits both you and your conflict partner.

3. Drawing on the Ladder of Assumptions tool explained in Chapter 1, make a preliminary study of the conflict by:

    *   creating a Ladder of Assumptions that you have climbed about your conflict partner, and by

- creating a Ladder of Assumptions you believe she has raced up about you.

- Note the guide for writing the Ladders, which follows.

My Assumptions About My Conflict Partner

Setting: How would I describe the backdrop for the conflict between us?

Facts: What are specific instances of my conflict partner's behavior toward me that are related to the conflict between us?

Interpretations: What personal characteristics of my conflict partner have been reflected in her behavior toward me?

Motives: Why has my conflict partner behaved toward me the way she has?

Generalizations: What stereotypes might I have applied to my conflict partner to explain her behavior toward me?

Actions: How have I been behaving toward my conflict partner since the conflict between us began?

My Conflict Partner's Assumptions About Me

(According To Me)

Setting: How would she describe the backdrop for the conflict between us?

Facts: What specific instances of my behavior toward her has she identified as being related to the conflict between us?

Interpretations: What personal characteristics of mine has she observed in the way I have behaved toward her?

Motives: What does she believe are the reasons why I have behaved toward her the way I have?

Generalizations: What stereotypes might my conflict partner have applied to me to explain the way I have behaved toward her?

Actions: How has my conflict partner been behaving toward me since the conflict between us began?

Putting Into Practice What You Have Been Learning

Part 2

4. Arrange a meeting with your conflict partner or, if a meeting with her isn't possible, arrange to have a phone conversation with her.

5. Begin the contact (meeting or phone call) with your conflict partner, with a statement something like: "I'm really concerned about the tension that I feel has been going on between us. I would like to do whatever I can to ease that tension so that hopefully it can go away. To do that, I need to know what you have been thinking about me and about our situation. So, can you help me by responding to some assumptions I have made about the tension?"

6. Hopefully, your conflict partner agrees to help you. If so:

   • Review with her the assumptions that you initially identified as ones she had made about you.

   • After you state each assumption to her, ask her whether the assumption you just stated is correct.

   • Listen carefully to your conflict partner's

assessment of the validity of each assumption you stated.

- Ask clarifying questions about any of her assessments that are initially unclear to you.

- Do not question the validity of her assessments.

- Thank her for being open and honest with her assessments of the assumptions that you had made.

- Acknowledge to her that you are going to make a sincere effort to understand her comments.

- After your meeting (or phone call), identify her assessments of your assumptions that, in your view, are grounded in reality. Make revisions in the assumptions that you originally believed she had made bout you.

- Based on her assessments that you believe are valid, make revisions in the assumptions that you originally felt she had made about you.

- Then, also based on her comments, make any revisions in the assumptions you have made about her that seem appropriate.

Putting Into Practice What You Have Been Learning

Part 3

7. Arrange another meeting with, or make another phone call to, your conflict partner.

- Thank your conflict partner again for her willingness to talk with you and to give you feedback regarding the validity of the assumptions you presumed she had made about you. Tell her that since then you have either discarded, or at least revised, those assumptions accordingly. Work together with her to decide which, if any, of those revised assumptions may still seem to be unfounded, and mutually let go of them.

- Then ask her if you can share with her the assumptions you have made about her. Hopefully, she will agree to allow you to do that.

- Listen carefully to your conflict partner's assessment of the validity of the assumptions you have made about her.

- Ask clarifying questions about any of her assessments that are initially unclear to you.

- Do not question the validity of her assessments.

- Thank her for being open and honest with you about her assessment of the assumptions you had made about her.

- Acknowledge to her that you are going to make a sincere effort to understand her comments.

- Following your meeting (or phone call), identify her assessments of the assumptions you had made about her that, in your view, are grounded in reality.

- Based on her assessments that you believe are based in fact, discard any assumptions you had originally made about her that are entirely unfounded.

- Then, make revisions in any of your assumptions about her that have at least some foundation to them.

- Make specific plans for scheduling another meeting with, or phone call to, your conflict partner to discuss with her your assumptions about her that you have either discarded altogether or at least have revised.

Putting Into Practice What You Have Been Learning

Part 4

8. Schedule another meeting with, or make another phone call to, your conflict partner.

   Discuss with her your assumptions about her that you have either discarded altogether or at least have revised.

   Finally, reach agreement with her on the assumptions each of you has made about the other that are based in reality.

9. Apologize to your conflict partner for any behavior on your part that has had an adverse impact on her.

   • If you didn't intend for your behavior to have an adverse impact on her, state that to her.

   • Tell her that you would like for the two of you to start fresh in your relationship.

   • Ask her if there is anything left in your about-to-be-resolved conflict that needs to be clarified before the two of you embark upon a fresh start.

   • Discuss with her anything she brings to light that needs to be clarified and ultimately agree with her on any clarifications the two of you reach, so as to remove any remaining obstacles to a fresh start.

10. Reach agreement on conditions in your relationship that both of you will follow so the fresh start on which you've agreed will be sustainable.

11. If neither meetings nor phone calls are possible with your conflict partner, accomplish the steps above by exchanging emails or letters with her.

12. When you have completed the steps above, write a summary of how you applied them in the conflict you had been having with your conflict partner, and the results of the efforts both of you have made toward achieving reconciliation.

REFERENCES

Adler, Ronald B., Lawrence B. Rosenfeld, Neil Towne, and Russell F. Proctor II. *Interplay: The Process of Interpersonal Communication.* Fort Worth, TX: Harcourt Brace & Company, 1998.

Allport, Gordon W. *The Nature of Prejudice.* Garden City, NY: Anchor Books, 1958.

Argyris, Chris. *Overcoming Organizational Defenses: Facilitating Organizational Learning.* Needham Heights, MA: Allyn & Bacon, 1990.

Bastis, Madeline Ko-I. *Heart of Forgiveness: A Practical Path to Healing.* Boston, MA: Red Wheel/Weiser, 2003.

Beer, Jennifer E. *The Mediator's Handbook.* Gabriola Island, BC, Canada: New Society Publishers, 2012.

Brady, Mark, ed. *The Wisdom of Listening.* Boston, MA: Wisdom Publications, 2003.

Covey, Stephen R.. *The 7 Habits of Highly Effective People: Powerful Lessons in Personal Change.* New York: Free Press, 1989.

Flanigan, Beverly. *Forgiving the Unforgivable: Overcoming the Bitter Legacy of Intimate Wounds.* New York: Macmillan, 1992.

Gladwell, Malcolm. *Blink: The Power of Thinking without Thinking.* New York: Little, Brown & Company, 2005.

Goleman, Daniel. *Emotional Intelligence: Why It Can Matter More Than IQ.* New York: Bantam Books, 1995.

_____. *Social Intelligence: The New Science of Human Relationships.* New York: Bantam Books, 2006.

Harris, A. H., et al. "Effects of Group Forgiveness Intervention on Perceived Stress, State and Trait, Anger, Symptoms of Stress, Self-Reported Health and Forgiveness" (Stanford Forgiveness Project at Forgive for Good at Learningtoforgive.com). Accessed February 24, 2012.

Haskins, Diana. *Parent as Coach: Helping Your Teen Build a Life of Confidence, Courage, and Compassion.* Portland, OR: White Oak Publishing, 2001.

Joint, Matthew. "Road Rage" for the Automobile Association Group Public Policy Road Safety Unit, AAA Foundation for Traffic Safety. Washington, DC: March 1995.

Accessed Feb. 16, 2012. http://www.aaafoundation. org/resources/index.cfm.

Jonick, Tony. "My Day as a Threat." *Perspectives*. San Francisco: KQED-FM, Feb. 19, 2008.

Katie, Byron. *I Need Your Love—Is That True?: How to Stop Seeking Love, Approval, and Appreciation and Start Finding Them Instead.* New York: Three Rivers Press, 2005.

Keltner, Dacher. *Born to Be Good: The Science of a Meaningful Life.* New York: W. W. Norton & Company, 2009.

Kottler, Jeffrey A.. *Beyond Blame: A New Way of Resolving Conflicts In Relationships.* San Francisco: Jossey-Bass, 1994.

Krumboltz, John D. and Al S. Levin. *Luck Is No Accident: Making the Most of Happenstance in Your Life and Career.* Atascadero, CA: Impact Publishers, 2010.

Lazare, Aaron. "Making Peace Through Apology," *Greater Good: Magazine of the Center for the Development of Peace and Well-Being,* Vol. I, Issue 2, Fall 2004, 16–19.

_____. *On Apology.* New York: Oxford University Press, 2004.

Lozada, Carlos. "Politically Correct, Linguistically Out-to-Lunch," *The Christian Science Monitor,* July 16, 1998, 16.

Luskin, Frederic. *Forgive for Good.* New York: HarperOne, 2001.

Patterson, Kerry, Joseph Grenny, Ron McMillan and Al Switzler. *Crucial Conversations: Tools for Talking When Stakes Are High.* New York: McGraw-Hill, 2002.

_____. *Crucial Confrontations: Tools for Resolving Broken Promises, Violated Expectations and Bad Behavior.* New York: McGraw-Hill, 2005.

Pearson, Peter, Cofounder, the Couples Institute. E-mail communication to authors. September 11, 2010.

_____. E-mail communication to authors. December 28, 2010.

Richo, David. *The Five Things We Cannot Change: And the Happiness We Find by Embracing Them.* Boston: Shambala, 2005.

Rodgers, Richard and Oscar Hammerstein II, "You've Got to Be Carefully Taught." Copyright © 1949 by Richard Rodgers and Oscar Hammerstein II. Copyright Renewed. International Copyright Secured. All Rights Reserved. Used by Permission of Williamson Music, A Division of

Rodgers & Hammerstein: An Imagem Company. From *South Pacific*, Act 2.

Rosenberg, Marshall B.. *Nonviolent Communication: The Language of Life*. Encinitas, CA: Puddle Dancer Press, 2003.

Ruiz, Don Miguel. *The Four Agreements: A Practical Guide to Personal Freedom*. San Rafael, CA: Amber-Allen Publishing, 1997.

_____. Don Miguel and Don Jose Ruiz. *The Fifth Agreement: A Practical Guide to Self-Mastery*. San Rafael, CA: Amber-Allen Publishing, 2010.

Sabee, Christina, Thom Massey, and Bea Herrick. *Mediation: Transforming Conflict Through Communication*. Thousand Oaks, CA: Kendall-Hunt Publishing, 2008.

Seligman, Martin E. P.. *Learned Optimism: How to Change Your Mind and Your Life*. New York: Vintage Books, 2006.

Senge, Peter M.. *The Fifth Discipline: The Art & Practice of the Learning Organization*. New York: Doubleday, 1990.

_____. Peter M., Art Kleiner, Charlotte Roberts, Rick Ross and Bryan Smith. *The Fifth Discipline Fieldbook: Strategies and Tools for Building a Learning*

Organization. New York: Bantam Doubleday Bell Publishing Group, 1994.

Stone, Douglas, Bruce Patton, and Sheila Heen. *Difficult Conversations: How to Discuss What Matters Most.* New York: Penguin Books, 2000.

Tannen, Deborah. *You Just Don't Understand: Women and Men in Conversation.* New York: Ballantine Books, 1990.

Tolle, Eckhart. *A New Earth: Awakening to Your Life's Purpose.* New York: Penguin Group, 2005.

Ueland, Brenda. *Strength to Your Sword Arm: Selected Writings.* Duluth, MN: Holy Cow! Press, 1992.

ABOUT THE AUTHORS

The four authors of *Conflict—The Unexpected Gift* are colleagues at the Palo Alto, California-based company Learn2Resolve, which specializes in helping clients resolve their conflicts.

Jack Hamilton has held positions as an instructor at Stanford University, a senior research scientist at the American Institutes for Research, and the director of executive services at the Institute for Information Management. He is a cofounder of the Information Group, Inc. He holds a bachelor of arts from Harvard University, a master of arts from the University of California–Santa Barbara, and a master of arts and a doctorate from Stanford University. He was honored by Santa Clara County, California, for his work as a mediator. He has taught conflict-resolution workshops at the Leadership Training Institute of the National League of Cities, as well as for businesses, nonprofits, and universities. He is the author of more than fifty journal articles and book chapters.

Elisabeth Seaman is a member of the Association for Conflict Resolution (ACR), the Association for Dispute

Resolution of Northern California, and the California Dispute Resolution Council. She has been conducting mediations since 1982. She mediates a wide range of disputes in commercial, community, workplace, real estate, consumer, family, interpersonal, and multicultural settings. She has facilitated meetings and led trainings in the United States, Mexico, and Costa Rica. She has taught conflict-resolution and communication-management workshops in commercial, public, and nonprofit settings. Elisabeth comes from a multicultural background, having grown up in Europe and Central America. She studied at the University of California–Berkeley for three years and completed her bachelor of science at Boston University.

Sharlene Gee holds a bachelor of science in electrical engineering and computer sciences from the University of California–Berkeley, and a master of science in electrical and computer engineering from UC–Santa Barbara. She has mediated disputes for more than ten years for the city mediation program in Mountain View, California, and for the Peninsula Conflict Resolution Center in San Mateo, California. She has taught conflict-resolution workshops at universities and at nonprofits and has led anger-management sessions at the San Mateo County (California) Women's Correctional Center. She was the 2006 recipient of the Gil Lopez Award, presented by the Association for Dispute Resolution of Northern California to "an individual person of color and/or multicultural team for creative interventions to conflict and violence."

Hillary Freeman earned a bachelor of science in marine biology at the Florida Institute of Technology, a master of science in fisheries biology at Iowa State University, a teaching credential from Notre Dame de Namur University, and a Google Fellowship. She has held positions as a lead scientist, computer programmer, and systems analyst. Following a career in sales management for the high-tech firm SAS Institute Inc., she was elected to a four-year term on the city council of Palo Alto, California. A trained mediator, she has taught conflict-resolution workshops at the Leadership Training Institute of the National League of Cities, as well as at businesses and nonprofits. She pioneered a conflict-resolution curriculum aimed at reducing the frequency of bullying among middle-school students.

CPSIA information can be obtained at www.ICGtesting.com
Printed in the USA
BVOW08s1210230215

388915BV00004B/10/P